D0321065

Soul at Work

Spiritual Leadership
in Organizations

Margaret Benefiel

QUAKER AUTHOR

VERITAS

Published 2005 by
Veritas Publications
7-8 Lower Abbey Street
Dublin 1
Ireland
Email publications@veritas.ie
Website www.veritas.ie

ISBN 1 85390 900 9

Copyright © Margaret Benefiel, 2005

Individuals portrayed in this book have consented to being
quoted and named. They do not necessarily represent
the views of the institutions with which they are affiliated.

The author thanks the editors of *The Leadership Quarterly* for permission
to use selected passages that originally appeared in different form in
"The Second Half of the Journey: Spiritual Leadership for Organizational
Transformation," *The Leadership Quarterly* 16, no. 4 (2005).

The material in this publication is protected by copyright law.
Except as may be permitted by law, no part of the material may be
reproduced (including by storage in a retrieval system) or transmitted
in any form or by any means, adapted, rented or lent without the
written permission of the copyright owners. Applications for
permissions should be addressed to the publisher.

A catalogue record for this book is available from the British Library.

CONTENTS

❦

Part One
FROM THE OUTSIDE IN

Part Two
AND BACK OUT

Part Three
PUTTING IT ALL TOGETHER

Foreword

The "Spirituality and Work" movement encompasses a new inter-disciplinary area of study. It draws upon theology, wisdom literature, metaphysics, mysticism, psychology, social psychology, sociology, biography, leadership, and organization studies. Small wonder as with most new intellectual syntheses, much of what is credible in this early period remains embedded in scholarly exchanges. Consequently, what is essential too often remains veiled behind the specialized languages of foundational disciplines. This leaves many frustrated practicing managers as well as students in higher education longing for a sensible distillation that is wise and readable without being simplistic.

Margaret Benefiel gifts us in *Soul at Work* with a perspective on the leadership dimension of this new area of study that cuts the Gordian Knot of complex conceptualization and esoteric language. Utilizing a limited number of business cases that contemporary organizational leaders will readily identify with, she gently opens the door to leadership spirituality. Each vignette contains rich exemplification that is memorable. Inferences are then carefully drawn regarding the spiritual journeys of leaders (part 1) and the impact on the overall organization (part 2).

Professor Benefiel is a knowledgeable theologian. She knows what to look for in the lived experiences of these leaders and their organizations in order to capture their spiritual journey. Then her theological insight enables her to provide lucid and tight reflections for both leadership and organizational culture. She does this well, but never drifts into esoteric theological or spiritual language. *Soul at Work* is a conversation regarding contemporary workplace spirituality that would be inviting in any company cafeteria or introductory university class.

Such clarity requires that the author be both wise and clear. Professor Benefiel is wise because she lets the manifestation of Spirit in each individual and organization speak for itself. In this she affirms that the Spirit blows where it will, and does so in the individuality and particularity of both person and organization. Yet she is clear because she is able to step back and provide theological interpretation and lessons provoking the reader to engage in careful reflection.

The novice needs such a guide to comfortably enter this important new literature. However, the book also holds great value for the well-read since the stories are vivid, illustrate first-order spiritual principles, and can be used as provocation for dialog at any level of depth or rigor.

Soul at Work is a good read for all of us interested in workplace spirituality. This perceptive little book invites the reader into a user-friendly conversation that contains memorable, grounded illustrations drawn from contemporary organizational life, focuses the reader on spiritual essentials, and allows the reader (or teacher) to probe at any depth that might be desired.

André L. Delbecq, DBA, FAOM, FACPE

Thomas J. and Kathleen L. McCarthy University Professor,
Leavey School of Business, Santa Clara University

ACKNOWLEDGMENTS

This book, even more than most, is the product of many people's efforts. I am grateful to the many people who opened their hearts, minds, and workplaces to me, generously giving of their time and thoughtfully reflecting on my questions. Thank you to all of you — I could not have written this book without you.

I am grateful to Beckey Phipps, with whom I discovered contemplative writing, co-authored two essays, and sowed the first seeds of this book. I am grateful to Linda Triemstra and the other staff of the Gordon Conwell Writers' Publishing Workshop, who taught me how to write a book proposal and believed in this book when it was merely the germ of an idea. I am grateful to the Lyman Fund and to Salem Quarterly Meeting of the New England Yearly Meeting of the Society of Friends, who awarded me grants to cover interview expenses. I am grateful to my agent, Sheryl Fullerton, who was a champion of this book from the beginning and who walked me through the vagaries of the publishing world. I am grateful to my editor at Seabury Books, Ken Arnold, who offered fine advice that helped make the book much stronger, and to his team, who did excellent and timely work every step of the way: Patti Byrns, Amy Davis, John Eagleson, and Parul Parmar. I am grateful to André Delbecq, mentor and friend, who has always inspired me with his spiritually grounded presence, even in the most difficult meetings, and who graced this book with a thoughtful and affirming foreword.

Eastern Point Retreat House in Gloucester, Massachusetts, provided a prayerful, inspiring atmosphere and excellent spiritual direction for week-long writing retreats during three different stages of the book. Friends generously prayed for and encouraged me, enduring my highs and lows through my e-mail updates and supporting me through thick and thin. Family and friends who read drafts offered many helpful suggestions and helped me see with new eyes—thanks to Susie Allen, Virginia Buck, Paula Hart, Joyce Gibson, Cynthia Knowles, Judy Locke, Diane Nettifee, Kara Newell, Debbie Spratley, and Paul Wagoner. Friends with whom I shared contemplative writing days helped me stay spiritually grounded and encouraged the first tender shoots of each chapter—thanks to Brita Gill-Austern, Monica Manning, Sile O'Modhrain, Sharon Thornton, and my steadfast writing friend, Cathy Whitmire. Pat Kelley and her team worked tirelessly to provide outstanding transcripts of interviews, often on short notice. Aer Lingus personnel, especially Elaine Doyle and Damien Duffy, helped ease the task of writing on the plane on my many long trips between Boston and Dublin. To each and every one of you, thank you so very much.

Most of all, I am grateful to my husband, Ken Haase, who faithfully edited drafts, encouraged me when my energy flagged, endured my preoccupation with this project, patiently put up with piles of papers in the dining room far longer than he should have had to, and loved me through the whole process.

Introduction

SOUL AT WORK

What do U2, Southwest Airlines, and Reell Precision Manufacturing have in common? They all manifest soul at work. Soul at work is not a theological abstraction or a dogmatic mantra, but the way that sustained purpose, culture, and identity can transcend and enhance an organization's performance and success. This book describes how soul at work functions in real organizations facing real issues. It describes the profound role that awareness of soul, or spirituality, can play in leadership and organizational life.

What is spirituality? For the purposes of this book, I define spirituality as "the human spirit, fully engaged."[1] Spirituality includes the intellectual, emotional, and relational depth of human character, as well as the continuing capability and yearning for personal development and evolution. In other words, this book considers spirituality in its broadest meaning, sometimes connected to religion, sometimes not. For example, at Southwest Airlines spirituality is not connected to a religion but manifests itself in humor, compassion, and relational competence. More traditionally, at Mercy Medical spirituality is connected to the charism of the Sisters of Mercy, called to serve the poor and underserved, especially women and children. The meaning of spirituality in an organization may also evolve, as in the case of Reell Precision Manufacturing, where the spiritual core of the company has been sustained while the outer words used to describe that core have expanded to be more inclusive of the growing organization. This book assumes that humans are inherently spiritual, and it examines spirituality as it is manifested in leadership and organizational life across a wide spectrum of organizations and traditions.

9

"Soul" is the lived manifestation of spirituality in an individual, a family, or an organization. It is the way that emotional or relational depth is honored and the way that yearnings for development or evolution are given space. A verb in noun's clothing, soul is how "the human spirit, fully engaged" is realized in the real world. Soul at work is the way that this manifestation exhibits itself in the world of everyday economic work and how purposes and practices combine to create a workplace that embraces fully engaged human spirits.[2]

The business case for soul at work has been well established.[3] Spiritually grounded organizations perform better and better enrich their stakeholders. They do this by sustaining economic profit, by building a reputation for quality and integrity in their products and services, by reducing employee turnover, by building long-term trusting relationships with customers and suppliers, and by giving back to the communities in which they live.

This book builds on the foundation of those books that have established the business case by examining stories and practical lessons of how soul appears at work in the organizations and leaders who manifest and sustain it. This book answers the questions, "What does soul at work look like?" and "How can I bring soul to work in my organization?"

This book is for those who suspect there is something more to business and organizational life than the financial bottom line. Not that the bottom line isn't important; it is foundational for the real work of the business: "Profit is to business what breathing is to humans. Both are essential to survival, but just as breathing is not the purpose of life, so profit is not the purpose of business."[4] This book tells the stories of businesses and other organizations that have found their purpose. It shows how they discovered that purpose and how they have lived out their purpose through the ups and downs of business cycles, through changing markets, through mergers, and through the stresses of globalization.

This is a book of stories—stories of people and of organizations, stories that seek to inspire, inform, and deepen. It helps those seeking purpose know they're not alone. It provides tools for the purpose-driven organization, tools that have withstood the test of time. It draws on deep spiritual traditions to unearth tools of discernment and spiritual guidance, demonstrating how those tools work and how they can be put to use in today's organizations. It shows real leaders and real organizations using spiritual discernment and experiencing transformation.

The seeds of this book were planted more than a decade ago as I taught at a theological seminary, preparing individuals to minister in churches across a range of denominations or to work in nonprofit contexts. As part of this preparation, students learned to care for their own souls amidst the tensions and demands of their everyday life and work. As I listened to and taught these individuals, I realized that something was missing. In particular, they were heading out to work in organizations which had their own issues and dysfunctions, but they were not being given tools to understand and sustain the souls of these organizations. They were being trained in individual spirituality, but not in organizational spirituality. At the same time, I realized that I, in the midst of my own institutional challenges, knew much about individual spirituality but little about how to bring those spiritual resources to bear on organizational life.

I began this book to fill that gap. I began by interviewing people at organizations which were explicitly spiritual. To my surprise, I soon discovered many people in business and other presumably non-spiritual settings who also hungered for spirituality in their work. As I examined various organizations, I found that the listening spiritual traditions in which I had been trained resonated with the organizational thinking which had started to emerge in business and management circles. I began to be invited to teach seminars and offer consulting in organizations that I had never dreamed would be interested in spirituality. As I offered what I knew about discernment, spiritual development, and spiritual guidance, I at the same time learned at least as much as I taught. I learned about business and organizational life. I learned the latest management theories. But above all, I met "ordinary saints," people who exercised spiritual practices and who underwent spiritual transformation in the midst of the nitty-gritty of daily business life. I learned from them how spirituality is relevant where the rubber hits the road, how spiritual practices can lead to individual and organizational transformation in the most unlikely settings. In all, I interviewed nearly three hundred people in businesses and other organizations, across the United States and in Ireland. In addition, I read materials written by the organizations, as well as materials written by outsiders about the organizations. While not all the interviews are included in this book, I have tried to take a representative sample of what I learned, articulating both the broad character and the personal experience of soul at work.

Organizations are created by individuals but necessarily transcend the individual as they act, grow, and evolve. This book is divided into three parts, reflecting (1) the individual role of leaders in nurturing soul at work, (2) the organizational reality by which soul is made manifest, and (3) the processes by which the tension between the individual and the organization are managed. Part 1 examines leaders, their leadership styles, their inner lives, and how they function in organizations. Part 1 begins with chapter 1 providing snapshots of soul at work in a range of organizations of increasing size: the U2 community, Sisters of the Road Café, Reell Precision Manufacturing, Greyston Foundation, HealthEast, and Southwest Airlines. Chapter 2 moves behind the scenes in four of these organizations, exploring the leadership that creates and sustains them. Chapter 3 answers the question, "How do those leaders do it?" by examining the inner lives of the leaders introduced in chapter 2. Chapter 4 considers the practice of spiritual discernment, demonstrating how discernment provides the foundation for leadership for transformation, giving examples from the lives of leaders introduced in chapters 1–3.

Part 2 moves from part 1's examination of leaders' styles and inner lives to considering the organization as a whole. It shows what soul at work looks like in action, in business and in nonprofits. It demonstrates how spiritually grounded leaders create and sustain spiritually grounded organizations. In order to be most practically useful, part 2 is organized according to the form of the various organizations and how their "soul at work" is stressed and sustained amid the conventional pressures and practices of their organizational life. Chapter 5 focuses on business, looking at Southwest Airlines and Greyston Bakery, both introduced in part 1, and adding a discussion of Document Management Group. Chapter 6 focuses on health care, concentrating on HealthEast, introduced in part 1, and adding a discussion of Mercy Medical and Our Lady's Hospice. Chapter 7 focuses on nonprofits, using the example of Sisters of the Road Café, introduced in part 1, and adding a discussion of Sophia Housing and the Shalem Institute. Chapter 8 then considers the practice of corporate discernment, building on chapter 4's introduction to individual discernment and giving examples from the lives of organizations introduced earlier.

The individual and the organizational, parts 1 and 2, draw together in chapter 9. Chapter 9 also demonstrates the relationship between the first half of the spiritual journey (when an individual or organization seeks spirituality for the tangible gifts to be gained) and the second half (when an individual or organization understands that the spiritual journey is more about its own transformation than it is about tangible gifts), drawing on the example of Reell Precision Manufacturing to illustrate this relationship.

From U2 to Reell Precision Manufacturing, then, soul at work transforms individuals and communities. The firstfruits of this transformation are increased productivity and satisfaction for stakeholders. As soul at work is sustained, the later fruit emerges: a concern for the transformation itself and a willingness to become the change one is seeking to make in the world. This concern creates the mix of commitment and resilience which can sustain the organization as assumptions, needs, and opportunities evolve. This book is about the ongoing process by which a concern for soul at work guides the coevolution of organizational soul and individual souls, and about what this coevolution looks like to its participants.

PART ONE

From the Outside In

Chapter 1

SOUL AT WORK

Six Who Manifest It

❊⟨◝⟩◜⟨◞⟩❊

THE U2 COMMUNITY

It's a very healthy way to live your life, not to be so wrapped up in yourself, but actually to think in terms of "us." I think U2 and U2's fans are good at thinking about "us" in a very broad sense.

This sense of "us," which the rock band U2's guitarist The Edge articulates, permeates all aspects of U2, from the way the band relates to one another, to the sense of community at U2 concerts, to the band's sense of connection with the wider world.

U2 (the band and the larger U2 community) is not your typical organization, but it clearly manifests the hallmarks of "soul at work." Behind the Grammy awards, the concerts, and the music, its members manage to create an identity that transcends the individual and supports the greater mission. This corporate identity has evolved from when the four band members first joined together in the 1970s and continues to evolve today. The challenge for U2, as for other organizations described in this book, is "How do we balance sustaining our soul, doing our work, and being individuals committed together?"

Within the band itself, huge rock star egos have no place. Band members ask themselves, "What's good for U2 as a whole?" While admitting that they all have quite healthy egos, The Edge observes, "Your ego, in our case, gets subsumed into a kind of band ego," a situation that is possible only because everyone is secure in his position. "No one's trying to do anyone else down. It's kind of the opposite. You know if you get a chance to compliment somebody else, in the end you're complimenting the whole band." The relationships band members have with one another stem from mutual respect and many years of hard work. Band members have grown up together, gone through their apprenticeship as musicians together, fought with one another, and matured in their Christian faith together. "There's a stability there and a kind of trust that is pretty indestructible at this point," comments The Edge. "A very miniature community like we have is a great model for success. It's a very effective form of cooperation for everybody involved."

Beyond the band itself, a sense of community pervades U2's wider circles. For example, The Edge notes, "At U2 concerts, there's a great sense of unity in the venue, whether it's a full stadium or a small theater. There's a kind of an understanding that everybody there shares a certain view of how the world could be, and they're interested in literally changing the world." Band members have been delighted to hear from such organizations as Amnesty International and Greenpeace that many new members have become involved with them because of U2's influence.

U2 members bring their whole selves to their music, including their spirituality, and thus go against the grain of the artistic world they inhabit. "We throw everything in, you know, politics, religion, sex, everything that is us. I think that is what's missing now in music, that completely holistic thing. It's like art and music mostly has completely turned its back on anything spiritual for such a long time," observes The Edge, also noting that he thinks that trend will change eventually. U2 is aware of a generation growing up in their native Ireland with the influence of the Catholic Church having waned and nothing yet replacing that spiritual influence. Because they believe that to be human is to be spiritual, U2 looks forward to the day when the spiritual element reasserts itself in Western society in general and in the arts in particular.

U2 members are not involved in the institutional church; they rely on their wider community to nurture them in their spiritual lives. The Edge describes this community: "There is that community sense that I would associate with the Christian ideal of looking after your neighbor. But it isn't always pretty; in fact it's often very rough. Like do you care enough about someone to risk confronting them with the truth, if it is going to hurt them? That's love in action, real commitment to one another, real community, and it has nothing to do with being nice to everyone at all times. So in some ways rather than being a once-a-week concept, it's sort of the way we try and live here. And the challenge is to try to move it out further, so there's not just your immediate small community but it's asking, can you get it to be bigger and bigger?"

While the band doesn't have a specific plan for increasing the scope of the good they do in the world, they continue to maintain their vision of transforming the world. And they know that that transformation begins with them. As The Edge puts it, "I just think by continuing what we're doing I hope there'll be a natural process of change in us." As they change, they understand that they'll influence the U2 community around them. The Edge muses, "It's nice to feel like you might have been a bit of a catalyst along the way, or to be more accurate, that the music and the culture that's grown up around the music would be a catalyst to other people to do something."

U2 incarnates what it is to think in terms of "us," in the band itself, in the U2 community, and in the wider world. In reflecting on the U2 community, The Edge typifies this attitude: "In the long run, I suspect that other people will end up doing far more than us, and that's an exciting idea."

SISTERS OF THE ROAD CAFÉ

"I need you. You are the social service center in the neighborhood. You can point me to where clothing is, you can point me to where the health clinic is, you can help me find a job. I know that about you. But don't you ever forget that you need me, too!" screamed the homeless woman who had burst into the staff meeting of the social service agency where Genny Nelson worked in 1979. The words struck home with Genny, reinforcing a message she had been hearing from the homeless for several years: "Listen to me. You need me."

Genny Nelson and her colleague Sandy Gooch founded Sisters of the Road Café in Portland, Oregon, in 1979, in response to hours and hours of conversation with homeless people, listening to them articulate what they needed in order to get back on their feet. They asked for an alternative to the missions and soup lines, a place where they could dine with dignity, a place where they could work for their meals. They asked for a safe space, for community, and for help in job training. "We don't want to be stuck in a lifetime of charity," they said.

Sisters of the Road became all that they requested, and more. Today, Sisters serves hot meals every day between 10:00 and 2:45. Customers can work for a meal or pay for a meal. They can work their way up to staff positions at Sisters. They can join the workforce development program and receive job training and help in job placement. The sense of community at Sisters is palpable. "This place is different," notes a customer. "You can feel it the minute you walk in the door." Customers and volunteers alike note the sense of respect and mutuality that pervades the atmosphere of Sisters of the Road. Not an easy atmosphere to maintain in the midst of the poverty and violence of life on the street, Sisters of the Road staff rely on their monthly nonviolence training and their daily practice of meeting violence with compassion to create and sustain the sense of community and mutuality at the café. "Nonviolence is the practice of living from the heart honestly," states Genny Nelson. "It asks of us the courage to address hurtful behavior while not humiliating that man, woman, or child's personhood." Genny attributes the atmosphere at Sisters to the consistency with which nonviolence has been practiced at Sisters over the twenty-five years of its existence.

At Sisters of the Road, staff, customers, and volunteers continue to work together to solve the problems of homelessness. The partnership between the homeless and the housed that Sisters conceived of initially continues in Sisters' day-to-day operations. "Listen to me! You need me." The message Genny received from the homeless woman who burst through the door has continued to echo in Genny's consciousness and has provided guidance throughout the years of Sisters' existence.

REELL PRECISION MANUFACTURING

> We are committed to do what is right even when it does not seem to be profitable, expedient, or conventional.

So reads the first principle in Reell Precision Manufacturing's Direction Statement. While such a principle might not appear to be a recipe for business success, Reell has grown from the 3-person company it was when it incorporated in 1970 to the 225-person company it is today. The company has adapted successfully to changing markets and a shifting economy and is now thriving, with revenue of over $25 million in 2004.

At first glance Reell seems as distant as can be from U2 or Sisters of the Road Café. What can a midwestern manufacturer of hinges and clutches possibly have in common with a rock band or a café for the homeless? Yet at the most fundamental level, as Reell's Direction Statement suggests, Reell shares a common core with U2 and Sisters of the Road. Reell, like U2 and Sisters of the Road, shares a commitment to soul at work, to manifesting its deepest values and its spirituality in its day-to-day life as an organization.

Reell discovered how to Enron-proof its organization long before American business knew how sorely such insurance was needed. Named after a German word meaning "honest" or "trustworthy," Reell made ethical behavior a part of its DNA from the start. Reell's first priority is the growth and development of its employees. Unlike most American manufacturing companies, who believe that workers must be constantly monitored in order to get the most work out of them, Reell believes in trusting its co-workers to do their best, thus freeing them to "express the excellence that is within all of us." Furthermore, Reell knows that business needs to make a profit, and they expect profits; at the same time, "our commitments to co-workers and customers come before short-term profits."

Because of its commitment to employees and customers, Reell has done such unconventional things over the years as limiting executive pay to roughly seven to ten times that of the lowest-paid employee. Furthermore, during economic downturns in 1975, 1979, and 2001, when other companies were laying off employees, Reell discovered another way and didn't lay off anyone.

"Do what is right, even when it does not seem to be profitable, expedient, or conventional" has served Reell well. By putting the development of their employees first and foremost, while at the same time keeping a steady eye on technology, markets, and the bottom line, Reell manages to work smarter, adapt quickly, and avoid the power struggles which often dominate technology and manufacturing companies.

GREYSTON FOUNDATION

I wanted to create an environment demonstrating the interdependence of life.... The big question was how to bring spirituality — an awareness of the oneness of life — to the marketplace.[5]

With these thoughts, Bernie Glassman recalls his motivation for founding Greyston Bakery, the forerunner to the Greyston Foundation (an umbrella organization for two for-profit ventures and five nonprofits) in 1982. While Glassman knew how to bring spirituality into nonprofits, he wanted to demonstrate how spirituality and commercial ventures could be linked. A Jewish astrophysicist turned Buddhist roshi, Glassman was influenced by both spiritual traditions when developing his principles of social engagement.

Greyston Foundation, located in Yonkers, New York, now includes not only Greyston Bakery but also Greyston Café, Greyston Family Support Services, Greyston Housing, Greyston Child Care Center, and Greyston Health Care. The bakery, currently a $5 million business, donates its profits to the Greyston Foundation to support Greyston's other projects. In addition to funding Greyston's nonprofits, the bakery contributes to Greyston's vision of social transformation by hiring "unemployable" people and training them to be successful.

While Glassman moved on in 1997, the spiritual foundation he put in place remains throughout all Greyston's branches. David Rome, one of those currently responsible for maintaining the spirituality of Greyston, serves as senior vice president for planning and development. Like Glassman, Rome grew up Jewish and later became a Buddhist. Rome attributes his spiritual formation to both traditions, and felt at home at Greyston when he arrived in 1992 because of Greyston's integration of Jewish culture and Buddhist practices. Rome seeks to help integrate spirituality throughout the internal organizational life of the Greyston Foundation, as well as throughout client services.

The various branches of Greyston have grown organically over the years as needs have become apparent. For example, Greyston Housing grew out of experiences at the bakery. Observing that many of the people who came seeking employment struggled with homelessness, Greyston leaders began exploring ways to address that problem. Greyston Family Support Services, in turn, grew out of these same explorations, as Greyston staff came to see that a more holistic approach to the problem of homelessness was needed than just providing housing. Greyston Family Support Services now provides everything from training in practical skills like budgeting and housekeeping to spiritual support for its tenants and prospective tenants.

Bernie Glassman's dream has been more than realized. Greyston has brought spirituality into the marketplace and has demonstrated the interdependence of life. From baking brownies to preparing homeless people to be housed, the Greyston Foundation demonstrates how soul at work can transform individuals and organizations.

HealthEast

> There's real compassion and love and relationship in this organization; there's friendship, there's support, there's trust. We have permission here to express ourselves in a different way.

With these words, Etta Erickson, program director for the cancer program at HealthEast, expresses her experience of the organization. HealthEast won the Best Minnesota Hospital Workplace award for

2003, based partly on HealthEast's employees' reporting descriptions of the organization similar to Etta's.

HealthEast was created twenty years ago through merging two Protestant and two Catholic hospitals on the east side of the Twin Cities in Minnesota. Now a health care system bridging two states, HealthEast boasts four hospitals, eleven clinics, five assisted-living residences, and various outpatient and home-care services.

HealthEast's "passion for caring and service"[6] shows up in how employees treat one another, in how employees treat patients, in the variety of support groups and therapies offered, and in the structures and processes of the organization. Staff at HealthEast work in interdisciplinary teams in order to build relationships across specializations and thus enhance staff relationships and patient care. Strengthened through a program called Interdisciplinary Clinical Practice, teams work regularly on improving the quality of their relationships and the quality of their patient care, measuring their results carefully.

HealthEast focuses on holistic patient care, offering not only state-of-the-art conventional medicine but also doing research on and offering alternative therapies such as healing touch and massage. In addition, HealthEast offers, as a complement to medical care, counseling and support groups on living with cancer, heart disease, diabetes, and other topics.

"Moments of Truth" at HealthEast are defined as moments when patients or their families have an opportunity to form an impression of HealthEast's service through contact with the organization. At HealthEast, employees remind one another that each "Moment of Truth" has the potential of becoming what they call a "Moment of Compassion." They notice and name "Moments of Truth" and share these stories with one another to encourage greater awareness.

The authentic relationships and compassion evident at HealthEast are examples of how a sustained commitment to organizational soul can avoid the stereotypical soulless bureaucracy which can emerge when institutions merge out of necessity. HealthEast's example demonstrates how a continuing focus on soul and relationship can help organizations and their cultures recover from the surgery of mergers and restructuring.

SOUTHWEST AIRLINES

In the midst of the failing U.S. airline industry, Southwest Airlines stands as a shining counterexample. The secret to its success? Fun.

When Rita Bailey, former director of Southwest's University for People, would frequently be asked about Southwest's employees, "How do you get people to do those fun things?" she would respond, "We hire fun people." Southwest flight attendants crack jokes during passenger safety briefings, pop out of overhead bins, and generally enjoy themselves in their work. Their attitude is contagious. Passengers enjoy flying Southwest Airlines, and go out of their way to buy their tickets on Southwest, where they consistently find the same attitude in flight attendants, ticket agents, gate agents, pilots, and ramp agents.

Since Southwest is known as a low-fare airline, its success is often attributed to its no-frills, point-to-point service. While these are important elements in its business model, they are not the most fundamental. Other airlines who have tried to copy Southwest focusing only on these elements have discovered that they can't compete.[7] Southwest's success depends on creating and sustaining fun, caring relationships — between top management and employees, among employees, and between employees and customers.

As Bailey says, understanding and living out Southwest's philosophy is "simple, but not easy." The fun at Southwest Airlines is not a superficial, irresponsible type of fun but is intrinsic to how employees connect to one other and to customers. One writer calls the secret of Southwest's success the power of "relational competence."[8] Simple to understand but not easy to live, relational competence requires both training and ongoing sustenance. Being caring toward fellow employees and customers is simple to understand but not easy to do in the relentless daily pressures of running an airline. It is because of these pressures that Southwest hires people who are already caring people

with a good sense of humor and then trains them to be even better at those skills. "You can teach behaviors that look like nice, but
that doesn't make me nice," observes Bailey. Southwest wants people
whose hearts are in their jobs and who are committed to living out
the philosophy of the airline.

The first airline to define itself as a customer-service business,
Southwest prides itself on its high customer-service ratings. Southwest is also the only airline to win the "Triple Crown" five years in a
row, based on the Department of Transportation statistics on on-time
arrivals, fewest customer complaints, and least misplaced baggage.

Financially, Southwest stands out against the backdrop of other
U.S. airlines, many of whom are losing money year after year and
some of whom are in and out of bankruptcy. Southwest, in contrast,
has turned a profit every year since 1973, and its stock is currently
worth more than all other major U.S. airlines combined.[9]

Building a business on fun may seem counterintuitive, but Southwest has demonstrated that, when understood in the right way, it
works brilliantly.

CONCLUSION

Organizations, like individuals, have souls that transcend and support their practical activity.[10] In these six organizational snapshots,
we have seen how that soul is manifest in a quality of care in personal relationships among the organizations' staff and stakeholders.
This quality of care is not blind to or divorced from bottom-line concerns, but it energizes individual and corporate activity toward those
concerns. Care of this kind is simple, but not easy in the real world
where decisions have to be made and deadlines need to be met. This
very tension is what makes organizational soul more than a Human
Resources policy; it is an insistence on holding the organization in
all its relational complexity while pursuing its economic, social, and
cultural goals. In the chapters that follow, we look more deeply at
the way in which soul at work manifests itself in these organizations
and others.

Chapter 2

BEHIND THE SCENES
Leadership for Transformation

꙳꙳꙳

You must be the change you wish to see in the world.
— GANDHI

Chapter 1 offered glimpses of six organizations manifesting soul at work. This chapter goes behind the scenes to observe what kind of leaders bring these organizations into being and sustain them over time. It introduces leaders from four of the organizations, showing the hows and whys of their leadership style and vision.

SISTERS OF THE ROAD CAFÉ: GENNY NELSON

"I need you, ... but don't you ever forget that you need me, too!" The message Genny Nelson received from the homeless woman recounted in chapter 1 became the foundation for Genny's philosophy of leadership at Sisters of the Road Café.

In 1972, when Genny Nelson was twenty years old and a student at Portland State University, she accepted a work-study job that changed her life. Two months after she began her part-time job working with homeless people in downtown Portland, she left her degree program at Portland State to pursue her work full time, and she has continued working with the same population for thirty-three years.

On her first night on the job in the homeless shelter, Genny looked around the large room filled with dozens of pallets and homeless men and asked in dismay, "What's a girl like me doing in a place like this?"

Desperate for help, she asked her co-worker what to do. He told her to listen to the men's stories and share her own, and she learned her first important lesson: leadership begins with listening.

Listening has served Genny well over the years. When she and her husband started Emmaus House of Hospitality and lived with homeless people for five years, she listened to their stories, learned from them, and was changed. Thus, when the screaming woman burst into the staff meeting in 1979, Genny knew the truth of her words and allowed them to lodge deeply in her heart. That woman's voice stayed with Genny as she and Sandy Gooch started Boxcar Bertha's, an information, referral, and advocacy center for women. Genny sought to listen deeply and respectfully to the women who came through Boxcar Bertha's, and in doing so she stumbled upon her next project.

That woman's voice also remained in her heart as Genny nurtured her next project. She and Sandy Gooch and the women who came to Boxcar Bertha's dreamed, envisioned, and finally founded Sisters of the Road Café, which has been serving Portland's homeless for over twenty-five years. "Homeless people need to have their voices in the search for solutions," claims Genny. Sisters of the Road Café emerged from over one hundred hours of conversations with the homeless. Women who came to Boxcar Bertha's told their stories, told their needs, told their desires and hopes. They shared their longing for a safe place for themselves and their children. They shared their desire for work experience and training. They shared their longing for a place to eat with dignity. As Genny listened deeply to the women's longings, Sisters of the Road Café was conceived and brought to birth.

Closely related to listening, empowerment likewise characterizes Genny's leadership: "When I have asked people in the café what can be done to eradicate their homelessness and poverty, they tell me that the biggest help is opportunity — education and systems that are set up to teach self-reliance, not dependence. They don't want to be stuck in a lifetime of charity." Honoring that, not only did Genny and Sandy listen to the homeless in founding Sisters of the Road, but they also +shared power and responsibility with them. Those who voiced the vision also played a role in bringing it into being. They helped select and ready the building, worked in the fledgling café, brought in art for the walls, and participated in planning and decision making. And Sisters continues as a partnership, empowering its customers. Since customers can either pay for a meal or work for a meal (there are no handouts at Sisters), each day's team of waitstaff, cooks, and cashier includes permanent staff, customers working for a meal, and volunteers. Each morning before the café opens, everyone who will be working that day gathers for a check-in. The group values everyone's input, and the entire group shares responsibility for running the café that day.

Not only can customers work for a meal, but they can also work their way up through the ranks. Customers can come through the door one day and work for fifteen minutes for a meal, and several months later work their way up to a permanent position. Both floor managers and cashiers have come in originally as customers. Furthermore, Sisters runs a workforce development program, helping place into other jobs workers who have come through the ranks at Sisters. The program offers mentoring and support as these workers make the transition to the outside world.

Genny is convinced that working in partnership is the only way the problems of homelessness will be solved. Only through enlisting the people most directly affected in the planning and problem-solving process can real change occur. For example, the Visions in Action project grew out of a period of brainstorming and planning, gathering together everyone interested in addressing the problems of homelessness. When all of the issues everyone could think of were listed on the walls, the group chose invisibility as the one to work on and planned the creation of a micro radio station. Homeless people who made the choice served as partners in carrying out their vision.

In addition to listening and empowerment, transformation characterizes Genny's leadership. She understands that practicing spiritually grounded leadership is about her own transformation as much as it is about what she offers her organization. Consistent with her deep listening and respectful empowerment, Genny bases her approach to transformation at Sisters on understanding how transformation occurs in herself: "Let's transform the world as we would transform ourselves." She notes that several elements occur in her transformation, and she builds the foundation of her approach to transforming the world on these elements. First, all people need compassionate allies. Second, all need decision making and values that include them. Third, everyone needs timelines that take into consideration the reality that most life changes don't happen quickly. Finally, everyone needs understanding and tender mercy when she or he makes mistakes.

Sisters of the Road Café, then, owes much of its character to Genny Nelson's leadership. As Genny leads with a commitment to listening, empowerment, and transformation, Sisters of the Road becomes the powerful transforming environment for which homeless people hunger. "Don't ever forget that you need me, too!" has served Genny well as a guiding principle.

REELL PRECISION MANUFACTURING:
BOB CARLSON

Like Genny Nelson's, Bob Carlson's leadership grows out of his own spiritual transformation. Also like Genny, Bob leads in a way that is integrally connected to his organization. Reell Precision Manufacturing (www.reell.com), a manufacturer of hinges and clutches located outside of St. Paul, Minnesota, claims at its heart the values of serving the common good and nurturing the growth and development of each employee (or "co-worker," as they are called at Reell). Bob Carlson, co-CEO of the company, holds in his heart his co-workers and the common good.

Bob searched for Reell for ten years: "I had been on a journey to start or find a business like this.... A lot of it has to do with working at a place that's congruent with my values and that reinforced and supported and even helped me grow in my sense of values and spirituality." As part of his journey, in 1992 Bob had clipped a newspaper column about Reell, stashing away the column with the thought,

"This is the kind of company I'd like to work for someday." When he interviewed at Reell six years later, having forgotten the specifics of the article, he began to think, "This sounds a lot like the company in the article I clipped," and he went home and found the article. Delighted, he discovered it was the same company. Bob and Reell found they were a good match. They carried the same values in their hearts.

What does Bob's leadership at Reell look like? How does Bob contribute to the atmosphere depicted in chapter 1? How does Bob's leadership at Reell help promote the growth and development of employees and contribute to the common good?

Bob lives Reell's values from the heart. Reell's Direction Statement begins with the injunction "Do what is right." "When we make decisions, the decisions aren't made through the filter of maximizing shareholder wealth. They're made through the filter of doing what is right," explains Bob. "We specifically ask the question, 'Who is affected by the decision, and is the decision good for all?' "

For example, during an economic downturn in early 2001, Reell leaders decided not to lay off anyone. First, they took profits down to zero. Then, when that wasn't enough, they asked everyone to take a pay cut. But rather than doing an across-the-board percentage pay cut, they did a graduated pay cut. Thus, Bob and his co-CEO took a 17 percent pay cut while most hourly workers took a 7 percent pay cut. Those who earned less than $11.40 per hour took no cut. Though times were tough, morale remained high. Bob described the co-workers' response: "When we called everyone together and explained the situation we faced, and then announced our graduated pay cuts, there were tears in people's eyes. They thanked us from the bottom of their hearts."

Furthermore, executive pay at Reell is modest to begin with. As a general guideline, the current CEOs are committed to receiving no more than six times the lowest pay of any employee who has been there five years and just ten times the lowest starting pay, in stark contrast to the eighty-to-one-hundred times ratio not uncommon in American companies today. "That just feels right," Bob explains. "It doesn't sit well with me to look at a company that I know has just gone through extensive layoffs in the past year and then read in the paper about the huge bonuses the executives got because they made more money that year."

A further way in which Bob's leadership at Reell helps promote the growth and development of co-workers is through the orientation and training that new co-workers receive. Bob and co-CEO Steve Wikstrom see that new co-workers receive two half days of orientation presenting Reell's identity and values. Co-workers hear about Reell's commitment to promote their growth and development and to contribute to the common good. They hear about Reell's commitment to "do what is right." Soon thereafter, they see these commitments in action when they receive Reell's TET (Teach, Equip, Trust) training. " 'The Teach, Equip, Trust' comes from the perspective that people are inherently good and inherently want to do a good job and that if they're not doing a good job, it's probably because they haven't been taught properly, not because of some fundamental lack of motivation," explains Bob. "A lot of it is really focused on freeing people. We try to remove the obstacles for people to be excellent. Let them know that they really have the freedom to go out and do the best job they can." The training focuses on giving people the tools they need to do their jobs and then letting them know they can ask for help whenever they need it, knowing that those they ask for help will be glad to give it. Thus, in addition to offering job skill training, TET imparts the culture of Reell. Employees learn that asking for help is seen as a positive trait, not a weakness. They learn that they are being liberated to be their best selves and that they will be trusted to do that. The result of this freedom and trust, remarkably, is discipline. Bob admits, "One of the things that continues to amaze me is how this company is self-disciplined. When somebody does go astray, it rarely comes to management. Peers self-discipline. Everybody enforces the standards."

Bob's heartfelt commitment to the common good and to the growth and development of co-workers is also demonstrated in his perspective on stock options. Currently he, Steve Wikstrom, and the cabinet, a senior management team of about fifteen, have stock options. In a recent board meeting, during a discussion about whether to extend stock options beyond upper management, Bob supported doing so. He explained that stock options represent more than just compensation. Because Reell is committed to the common good, stock options might be considered "sacred trust shares." Stewardship of Reell needs to be entrusted to those who will "do what is right." Bob explained that they would say to co-workers, "The real reason we're giving this to you is because you're part of the group we're entrusting this company to. You would become a significant part of ownership to help us be faithful to who we are."

Finally, Bob is committed to "doing what is right" by serving customers well, even when the cost is high. He tells stories of Reell inviting customers into conversations about what to do with a product that has already been shipped when potential flaws have been discovered. A 1991 product recall cost Reell over fifty thousand dollars. On another occasion, when a customer in Taiwan needed a product the next day, a Reell employee flew to Taiwan to deliver it personally. Bob Carlson is committed to maintaining a company that does what is right "even when it does not seem to be profitable, expedient, or conventional."

At the heart of Reell, then, is its commitment to "do what is right" for its employees and for the common good. Because Bob Carlson holds Reell's employees and the common good in his heart, he and the company are a good match. His heartfelt commitment keeps Reell aligned with its values in all aspects of its daily operations.

GREYSTON FAMILY SUPPORT SERVICES: THERESA McCOY

Compassion is the hallmark of Theresa McCoy's leadership. As former director of Greyston Family Support Services in Yonkers, New York, Theresa leads with compassion, vision, a light touch, and deep groundedness in the midst of turmoil. She "looks beyond her eyes."

Transformation occurs around her. Theresa's compassionate leadership manifests itself in three intertwined arenas: community building, training, and organizational nurturing.

Theresa built community as she directed the support services for tenants of Greyston Housing, a fifty-one-unit apartment complex housing formerly homeless people, primarily single mothers. Much of her community-building work focused on creating situations in which clients could hear one another deeply across their differences. Theresa maintains that beneath the racial, ethnic, and spiritual diversity among the women with whom she worked, her clients shared similar hopes and dreams, needs and longings. She sought to help them discover and share their spiritual core, and in so doing she built support systems. Theresa knew that she couldn't be afraid of hard questions. When one of her clients asked, "If I don't believe in God, does that mean I'm not spiritual?" Theresa welcomed the question as an opportunity to explore spirituality more deeply, helping women who inherited an authoritarian view of God find their own way and respect one another's different paths.

Theresa's community building continued in the training program she directed. Before tenants move into Greyston housing they receive training, meeting twice a week to focus on basic life skills and spiritual development. Theresa selected tenants and designed and facilitated the program. Throughout their four months of meeting together, Theresa sought to empower prospective tenants and build community. In the training she offered, Theresa focused on problem solving together, creating structures for dialogue and relationship.

During the four-month training program, one of the two weekly meetings focused on life skills such as housekeeping and budgeting. The other meeting, called the Pathmaker meeting, focused on helping each participant identify and travel her own spiritual path. At the Pathmaker meetings, Theresa facilitated a Native American process called the Way of Council. Participants sit in a circle and pass around a talking piece, a stone taken from the building they will inhabit, speaking only when they have the talking piece and leaving a respectful silence between speakers. Participants learn five practices:

listening from the heart, speaking from the heart, spontaneity, being of lean expression, and confidentiality. As these homeless women prepare to be housed, they share their struggles with one another, and in the process, they learn how to share and listen deeply. They learn how to ask for and receive support. They gain not only external skills but also internal strength. They learn that this environment encourages exploration and questioning of spiritual assumptions, something many of them have never done before: "Primarily the population that we served are women of color.... Having family members from the South and being a woman of color myself, I was raised, 'There's God, and that's it.' " As Theresa learned to question her own assumptions and discover her path, so she taught prospective tenants to discover their paths. Theresa found great joy in her work, especially in the spiritual aspect: "I say this not to in any way dilute the significance of attaining jobs ... and other kinds of earthly advances, but my greatest success is to see the internal change that has manifested in individuals based on their understanding of their spiritual self in a different kind of way. That's the achievement. That's what motivates me to get up in the morning."

Theresa continued to facilitate tenants' meetings after tenants moved into Greyston Housing. Tenants continue to develop life skills, support one another's spiritual growth, and build community with one another. Theresa taught the women, "If you can see it, you can do it. You can achieve it if you can see yourself there." As they grew in their skills, the women took on more responsibility, gradually assuming Theresa's tasks.

Finally, Theresa's compassionate leadership manifested itself in her nurturing of the organization as a whole. Theresa knows that nurturing spirituality in the workplace makes a difference: "Does spirituality increase productivity? Well, if you're happy, if you feel centered, if you're at peace, you're going to rock. If you're miserable, if you're in conflict with self and others, not a whole lot of work is going to get done." At Greyston, she discovered a place where her efforts to bring spirituality into the workplace were welcomed: "This is the only job I've had that really has a respect for spirituality in the workplace, and there's quite a difference. I've worked with the developmentally disabled, I've worked with the emotionally disturbed, I've worked with ex-offenders. And in all of those populations in the past that element was not there, and it was sorely needed. Sorely needed." According to Theresa, the underlying difference is compassion. In an organization grounded in compassion, everyone has a sense of mission. Everyone has a sense of responsibility. Everyone's gifts are recognized and encouraged, and there's a sense that the whole is greater than the sum of its parts. "You feel differently about who you are in relationship to the whole."

At the same time, Theresa is the first to admit that Greyston is not perfect: "I would not want to portray an idealistic utopia, because a utopia it's not, but the foundation is there." She acknowledges that staff and residents all struggle with how to integrate spirituality into organizational life: "It's difficult because we are an agency that has all the constraints of any other agency. We don't exist in a vacuum." They struggle with how a hierarchical structure can coexist with spirituality in the workplace. They struggle with how the deadlines of funding agencies can coexist with spirituality in the workplace. They struggle with how the pressures of overwork and demands from multiple constituencies can coexist with spirituality in the workplace.

While the struggles continue, Theresa's compassionate leadership has left its mark. As Theresa met impossible challenges with compassion for her clients and for her co-workers, clients and co-workers alike acknowledged the difference in atmosphere, energy, hopefulness, and joy.

HealthEast: Joe Clubb

Like a gardener, Joe Clubb seeks fertile ground for planting seeds. In HealthEast, he found it. Joe found in HealthEast an organization that reflected his values and had committed itself to putting them into practice. He found fertile ground for planting seeds of spirituality.

Joe came to HealthEast in 1995 as one of three service line directors of social work and soon became head of social work services for the entire four-hospital system. HealthEast's commitment to spiritually based values drew Joe initially and kept him there as he discovered the depth of that commitment. Early on, Joe noticed employees' comfort with prayer at all levels of the organization and realized that his gift for nurturing prayer in meetings and one-to-one relationships would be welcomed. At the same time he noticed the willingness of staff to call on social workers for spiritual care of patients in addition to their specified task of discharge planning, thus acknowledging the possibility of integrating social work and spirituality, an integration he had heard espoused in other contexts but had never before seen practiced.

These as well as other observations let Joe know early on that he could bring his whole self, spirituality and all, into the workplace at HealthEast, and he began to dream about how he could fully practice the kind of leadership he had always wanted to try.

What does Joe's leadership at HealthEast look like? Like a gardener, Joe envisions the big picture and at the same time plants seeds and tends shoots. For example, three years into his job, Joe heard a presentation about Interdisciplinary Clinical Practice (ICP),[11] a method of integrating spirituality into patient care, and he, along with a number of others, immediately recognized it as a tool that could help HealthEast put its principles more fully into practice. Joe and others received ICP training, and Joe saw the potential for ICP, originally conceived as a model for nurses, to be extended beyond nursing teams. With this vision for the big picture, and working jointly with Pattie Keefer, RN, Joe assumed primary responsibility for bringing ICP into widening circles of patient care at HealthEast.

Based on two tenets — reminding a health-care organization of its purpose and the valuing of relationships — ICP practices help employees "walk the talk." Putting the first tenet into practice involves beginning each meeting (or "council" in ICP language) with a patient story, orienting the council toward its ultimate purpose, the care of a patient's body, mind, and spirit. Someone shares a story of a patient on that particular nursing unit who has been helped by HealthEast. Putting the second tenet (valuing relationships) into practice involves basic ground rules for the council: issues discussed come from staff rather than administration, a staff person rather than the director of the unit facilitates the council, no one dominates, and participants share their lives with one another as well as doing business.

Not only did Joe plant seeds and tend shoots as he helped establish ICP on the nursing units, he also dreamed big about how to extend ICP beyond its original scope. First, he helped establish interdisciplinary councils on the nursing units. Next, Joe suggested that a council be composed of the entire team that works on the unit. Thus one council might include a dietitian, a social worker, and a housekeeper, as well as nurses. Furthermore, while ICP focuses on considering the patient as a whole person, body, mind, and spirit, Joe suggested that HealthEast teams add another component: seeing *themselves* as whole people. Thus, team members take turns at council meetings sharing spiritual reflections from their experience, building a foundation of spiritual community with one another.

Second, Joe helped establish broader councils throughout the hospitals. Since not all employees involved in patient care work on nursing units, not all had the opportunity to participate in a council. To make the interdisciplinary process available to all staff members, Joe set up councils throughout the HealthEast system. For example, the oncology leadership council consists of leaders across HealthEast who work in oncology, including representatives from chemotherapy, radiation, hospice, palliative care, and social work. Such councils helped spread the ICP practices into all aspects of patient care. In addition they cultivated an atmosphere of interconnection among HealthEast employees, helping people see one another as teammates rather than strangers or, worse, competitors.

Like a gardener, Joe recognizes that growth occurs organically. While he can envision the whole and plant seeds, his subsequent work involves attending to what grows naturally. He realizes that the process of growth in the garden is bigger than he is and that his job is to stand in awe of the process and tend the shoots as they emerge. Thus, with ICP, Joe looks for fertile ground where he might sow ICP seeds, then observes where the practices take root and grow, and then does what he can to encourage growth in those places.

Because of Joe's leadership with ICP, he was invited to head a strategic planning process for St. Joseph's Hospital, one of the hospitals of HealthEast. Joe led the strategic planning team, first, by nurturing the spiritual foundation of the group. Ample time was given in meetings for spiritual sharing and listening. The insights that emerged from this time were taken seriously. Furthermore, the team reflected on the ways in which spirituality already undergirded so much of the work at St. Joseph's, in its stated mission and in practice. As they celebrated the spirituality already present, they dreamed about how that spirituality could be brought more fully into the hospital as a whole. Out of this work emerged a plan for introducing ICP to areas beyond patient care, such as human resources and corporate services.

In all aspects of his leadership at HealthEast, then, Joe acts as a faithful gardener. He dreams about the whole, plants seeds, nurtures connections, appreciates organic growth, and supports the shoots as they emerge.

CONCLUSION

These four leaders, different in background, spiritual tradition, and work setting, share a common core: they manifest soul at work and they lead their organizations through spiritual transformation. They know that the spiritual journey is more about their transformation than it is about the gifts they receive, and they know that the organizational spiritual journey is more about the organization's transformation than it is about material rewards. While all four of their organizations have thrived under their leadership, these leaders know that material success, while it is one element of a healthy organization, is not the most fundamental. Because their leadership grows out of a wellspring of deep spiritual groundedness, their leadership is characterized by compassion, service, respect, and wisdom. Paradoxically, keeping their eyes on the spiritual goal often results in material reward.

Chapter 3

LEADING FROM THE INSIDE OUT
The Inner Life of the Leader

⁙❦⧽⧼❧⁙

Chapter 2 considered what soul at work looks like in a leader, showing how a spiritually grounded leader acts in various situations and
what a spiritually grounded leader contributes to an organization.
What goes on inside such a leader? What kind of inner life makes it
possible for the leader to lead an organization through spiritual transformation? This chapter considers the inner lives of the four leaders
introduced in chapter 2.

GENNY NELSON: INNER NONVIOLENCE

For Genny Nelson, inner nonviolence is primary. Out of the core of
inner nonviolence radiates the outer nonviolence she practices in her
personal life, in Sisters of the Road Café, and in the wider world.
But sustaining this inner nonviolence as Genny attentively listens to
and empowers homeless people day after day is not easy work. Being
open to transformation in the midst of the crucible of violence and
poverty may sound like a beautiful ideal, but the daily reality of transformation discourages even the noblest of souls. How does Genny do
it? By maintaining a strong inner life. She finds her strength in two
places: God and spiritual community. "I don't do this work by myself. I could not do this work without my faith in God." She keeps an
ongoing conversation with God throughout the day, constantly turning to God in the midst of the challenges she encounters. She keeps a
journal, recording her inner thoughts and feelings and prayers. Her
journal helps her notice how God is at work in her life and work,

and it also helps her in her discernment. In addition she takes other time alone with God, apart from her daily responsibilities, when she needs it. The downtown chapel, one of her favorite spots for getting away to pray, frequently provides her with the respite she needs. "I have my own little prayer, and it's, 'I'm laying it at your feet.'" For example, "One time at the café we had less than one hundred dollars in the bank account. I landed in the downtown chapel, and I just started crying and said, 'I'm a really stubborn woman. If you don't want me to do Sisters anymore, I'll get that, but you gotta give me a big sign, like put it on a billboard: Genny, stop doing Sisters.'"

In addition to her personal time with God, Genny relies on her spiritual community as a source of strength, courage, and compassion. Genny grew up Catholic, and the Catholic Worker movement strongly influenced her. The Catholic Worker philosophy of nonviolence and gentle personalism inspired Sisters of the Road's philosophy. The Catholic liturgy with which Genny feels most at home now is the Mass at the downtown chapel. These days Genny finds her spiritual community at Sisters of the Road. "I feel like there is a community of faith at Sisters, and that nourishes me." Earlier in her life, when she worked at a social service agency, Genny felt that she was working *for* people, and that work drained her. Now, "when I work alongside *with* people, . . . it just gives back. The center of my heart is Sisters of the Road."

Genny's leadership transforms others and society, and she is transformed in the process. From her first day on the job in the homeless shelter, to her five years of living with the homeless at Emmaus House, to her twenty-five years at Sisters of the Road, Genny has listened and learned and been changed: "I am a better woman, I am a stronger woman, for all the stories that people who are different from me have let me be a part of."

The philosophy of nonviolence calls upon its practitioners to meet violence with consistency, firmness, and love. In so doing, Genny encounters the violence within herself. Time and again, she has had to see the violence, racism, and domination within herself and choose to respond with compassion toward herself and toward the other. "As long as our country continues on a violent path of racism and classism, I will never be able to say as a white and privileged woman, 'I am not racist, I am not classist.' I must steadfastly work on my racism and every other kind of violence that rears up in me." The staff meets monthly for nonviolence training, to support one another in meeting with love the violence they encounter in the café daily. In so doing, they share their awarenesses about the violence within themselves that gets triggered by the outward violence they encounter, and they support one another in meeting with love the violence within. "We share a common woundedness and a mutual responsibility with our customers. None of us has a monopoly on the truth." The outer violence continually challenges Genny to deepen her inner nonviolence. Her nonviolent core gains strength through her daily encounters with violence. Genny's spiritual practice of meeting violence with compassion has opportunity to be exercised daily, and her nonviolent core grows strong enough to meet the next challenge of violence. The process nurtures itself.

BOB CARLSON: DEEP-FLOWING STREAM

Bob Carlson's inner life, like a deep-flowing stream, keeps his leadership vital. Like a stream, his inner life is fed by many sources, inside and outside of Reell.

Outside Reell, Bob finds that sabbath time, whether in the form of walking alone in nature, music, or worship at his Protestant church, feeds his soul. Because he thinks that busyness is the biggest enemy of spirituality, Bob seeks sabbath time wherever he can find it. As co-CEO of Reell, Bob finds that his life easily gets filled with too much activity, from the daily internal demands of Reell to extra meetings and outside activities. The busier his life becomes, the harder it is for him to be in touch with the deep-flowing stream within. Bob's most consistent sabbath time comes in walking, especially walking alone in nature: "There's just something about getting connected to the earth — I can feel myself slowing down, and I can feel the blood pressure dropping." Walking reconnects him to the stream within and gives him fresh perspective on his responsibilities. Listening to music is another form of sabbath for Bob. Whether it's traditional church music during Sunday morning worship, music in the car during his daily commute, or putting on a CD at home and taking time to relax and let the music take him wherever it will, Bob finds that music nourishes his soul.

Within Reell, Bob finds spiritual nourishment as well. Weekly Tuesday morning breakfast meetings with co-CEO Steve Wikstrom and board co-chair Bob Wahlstedt regularly provide Bob with "inspirational wisdom." Informally named after the fourth direction in Reell's Direction Statement ("Seek inspirational wisdom"), the breakfast meetings "begin with meditation time . . . and quite often the conversation will go in a religious or spiritual direction," reports Bob. The meetings always conclude with seven minutes of silence, time to listen for God's voice and to the deep wisdom within, in the midst of the many conversational threads that have arisen. Though the men give themselves permission to talk about whatever comes up, including things that have nothing to do with the business, they often discover during these meetings spiritual insights into issues facing the business. In addition, they reconnect with one another spiritually, thus refreshing the spiritual foundation of the corporate life of their triad.

To his surprise, Bob has also found Reell board meetings to be occasions for vulnerability and spiritual support. On his second day at Reell Bob attended a board meeting that opened with a video of the poet David Whyte reading poetry to a corporate audience and drawing meaning relevant to business from it. "I remember sitting there thinking, 'Boy, this wouldn't happen in many places. Not too many businesses want David Whyte at the beginning of a board meeting.'" Bob found Whyte's poetry very moving and learned that board meetings at Reell would welcome spiritual reflection and emotion. A year later, in the course of making a presentation to the board about an employee who had died and how the company had responded, Bob broke down: "It just hit me. Well, I didn't feel embarrassed, and I think I would have felt embarrassed in other places I'd worked because I would have known that you don't do this at work. But here our emotional self is okay whatever that is and that sadness, that grief, you know, you don't get to plan for when that's going to show up." The board members appreciated Bob's openness and the opportunity to share in his grieving process, and Bob felt supported by them.

Finally, Bob finds in the atmosphere of Reell support for the growth and nurture of his inner life. At other times in his life Bob describes himself as having gone from being in a state of spiritual oasis to being in a spiritual desert, but, "It's hard to do that at Reell because collectively the way we bring a spiritual perspective to so many of the things we do results in spiritual growth for me." Working at Reell helps keep him out of the spiritual desert. For example, Bob found the early 2001 economic slowdown and Reell's response to it to be one of those growth-producing experiences. Though it was a difficult challenge to meet the 30 percent drop in revenues with appropriate budget cuts, Bob appreciated the opportunity to discuss with others on the Reell management team what it would mean to "do what is right." As the group decided on graduated pay cuts instead of layoffs, Bob saw the decision-making process work well, the decision boost co-workers' morale, the subsequent months' revenue return wages and salaries to their previous level, and the skeptics convinced. He found that the process helped him grow personally, both in trust of his colleagues and in trust of the process.

Time and again, Bob has been challenged to grow at Reell. "Reell talks about being about the growth and development of people, and I think most of us think of that more in terms of the rank and file and not so much about someone who is co-CEO. But I really feel that it has worked for me, too, and I think I'm a better person than I was several years ago when I started." Through being challenged to live up to the vision of Reell's Direction Statement and through being with others who are doing the same, Bob has grown stronger in his core and has found his heart expanded. "The need to be faithful to our values and principles, to the Direction Statement and Declaration of Belief, and having to frame decisions, more so than I've ever had to do in my life, with those perspectives, has made me a better person."

THERESA MCCOY: COMPASSION

Theresa McCoy, former director of Greyston Family Support Services, frequently found herself in demanding situations. She discovered that returning to her spiritual center provided her with the wisdom, courage, guidance, strength, and compassion she needed to make the impossible possible.

Founded on Buddhist principles, Greyston Family Support Services integrates spirituality into all levels of its structures and processes. A Nichiren Daishonin Buddhist herself, Theresa emphasizes the importance of spirituality and the importance of inclusiveness. While Greyston staff encourage the spiritual development of their clients, they do not seek to make everyone Buddhist. They stress the importance of each person's discovering and following her own path.

Because Theresa has intentionally followed a spiritual path for over thirty years, she has a storehouse of experience to draw upon. It hasn't always been easy. This is what she brings to her work: "Spirituality is an understanding that everything is transient and there is a more expansive relationship and responsibility that we have to ourselves and to others that we must ultimately respect."

How does Theresa draw on this storehouse of spiritual experience and on this understanding of spirituality? How did it inform her day-to-day leadership at Greyston? First, she approached her work as an ongoing opportunity for spiritual growth. For example, Theresa viewed her position at Greyston as an opportunity to understand herself more deeply. "I truly believe that my environment is a reflection of what is in my own life, and it's my role to serve people and in turn serving myself and appreciating the God in me. . . . Since the environment is a reflection of oneself, I have encountered a reflection of myself through the work that I have done: I have seen my anger, I have seen my sadness, I have seen my suffering." As she sees these parts of herself and finds the courage to face what's within, she finds that she can help others do the same. For example, she found herself saying to herself in a meeting, "I really don't like that person. She's so opinionated. How disgusting!" After praying about her reaction, she realized, "Ahh, *I'm* so opinionated," acknowledging that what she didn't like in the other person was what she didn't like in herself. Through viewing her life experience as a mirror in which to see herself, Theresa continues to grow spiritually.

Second, when she needs help, Theresa prays. For example, she had a tenants' meeting that lasted until 11:30 p.m. one night and left her distraught. She went home and prayed and slept, but morning came too quickly, with another series of meetings, and she felt very stressed. She made it to work, but knew she wasn't in any shape to go into another meeting. So she decided to take a prayer break at work: "Before the meeting, I went into my office, and I rang my bell and prayed. The prayer is not a silent prayer, it's quite vocal, and it really is pulling up all that negativity, to be able to say, 'It's okay, it's good that you're going through this challenge in your life. . . .' That's what we aspire to, to ultimately look at life's challenges and to be able to say, 'Okay, this person really was very unkind to me' and not. 'I would like to hit them' or, 'I don't like you,' but to actually say, 'Thank you. Thank you very much.' " Through turning to prayer, she was able to let go of the accusations and hurts of the night before, to recenter and go into her meeting with equanimity and compassion.

Third, Theresa's spirituality helps her let go of blame and take responsibility for her life. "We're not really conditioned in this society to look at ourselves as well as the other guy. One of the things I talk to a lot of people of color about is, when are *we* going to stop pointing the finger and take responsibility for our own lives, when are *we* going to start owning and loving our own lives?" Theresa believes that part of spirituality is taking responsibility for her life, seeing her life as a gift that is temporary. And she believes that part of her responsibility is to address past hurts and injustices in her life: "There are some things I need to turn around in my life to change poison into medicine."

Though Theresa had sought to develop her spiritual life and bring her spirituality to bear on her leadership for many years, Greyston was the first place she worked where she had explicit support for this endeavor. She appreciated the atmosphere at Greyston, an atmosphere that reminded her to turn to her spiritual resources in the midst of the leadership challenges she faced. For example, when she would recount her difficulties in a staff meeting, "It wouldn't be unheard of for the president to ask me, if I was complaining about having a really hard day, 'Did you pray about it?' "

JOE CLUBB: PRAYER

Like Theresa McCoy, Joe Clubb relies on prayer. In fact, in his early days at HealthEast, he relied on it desperately. His new responsibilities represented a stretch from his previous job, and he found himself turning to God frequently. He often felt that divine guidance provided him with a way through a difficult meeting or a sticky personnel situation. In addition, he learned that he could rely on the prayers of others. When faced with a tough situation, Joe would ask a colleague to pray for the situation to help him through it. For example, "As groups went through the forming, storming, norming kind of group process, I asked for prayer for the more difficult times."

Now, in his demanding job as director of social work for the HealthEast system, Joe views his spiritual life as his foundation for giving to others. Furthermore, he creates space for his co-workers to nurture their spiritual lives, claiming, "We have to take care of ourselves spiritually if we are going to be present to our patients and families spiritually."

Joe receives regular spiritual sustenance in a number of ways. More formally, in addition to regular worship at his home Catholic parish where he serves as a cantor, Joe attends Mass regularly at St. Joseph's Hospital, worshiping with his colleagues, patients, and patients' families. In addition, due to his faithful work of bringing ICP to HealthEast, spirituality infuses his work setting, and he receives spiritual sustenance there. Council meetings at HealthEast begin with prayer for guidance, and a prayerful spirit permeates the meetings as all participants share from their spiritual experience and listen deeply to one another.

More informally, Joe doesn't hesitate to ask spontaneously for prayer from colleagues when he faces a particularly difficult situation. For example, recalling a recent stressful meeting, Joe recounts calling a colleague to ask for help in thinking through how to facilitate it and then asking her to pray for him at 12:30, when the meeting would begin. She called him back later to ask how the meeting had gone and to share how she had prayed for him, adding, "I love this organization because we are comfortable enough to be able to ask each other for prayer and say prayer with each other." Joe relates, "You know, that meeting went extremely well, and I know it was because of that divine intervention." Joe counts many of his colleagues as potential prayer partners, saying how he will run into someone in the hall and ask for prayer or call any of a number of people with prayer requests.

As chair of the strategic planning committee, Joe has integrated prayer into the group's process. Meetings begin with prayer for guidance. Members of the committee share their spiritual lives with one another and learn to listen to God together. Joe also seeks ongoing prayer from others outside the committee, believing that a foundation of prayer is just as important a part of strategic planning as careful facilitation of meetings or broad information gathering. For example, early in the process he visited two related bodies to lay out his vision for the strategic planning process and to ask for their ongoing prayers. First, he visited the vice president of spiritual care for HealthEast, outlining his vision, seeking counsel, and requesting a commitment of prayer. Joe offered to give regular progress reports, making clear how important the contribution of prayer would be to the process. Second, he visited the Sisters of St. Joseph leadership team. Since the Sisters were celebrating 150 years in the Twin Cities, looking back over the work they had done in that century and a half, and since St. Joseph's was one of the hospitals they had founded, Joe wanted to enlist their prayer support. As St. Joseph's moved into its next chapter of serving the area, the Sisters' prayers would be an important investment in the strategic planning process.

CONCLUSION

Genny Nelson's inner nonviolence, the deep-flowing stream Bob Carlson draws upon, Theresa McCoy's compassion, and Joe Clubb's prayer all constitute the core of a person who leads. Like the external manifestations of their leadership, the internal core of these leaders is different yet the same. Their differences in background, religious tradition, gender, and race notwithstanding, these leaders share a common core. Rather than leading out of domination or outward strength, these leaders lead from quiet internal strength and integrity. Because the leadership challenges they face are some of the toughest around, they need the strongest, most resilient kind of leadership possible, and all of them have found what they need in the practice of spiritually grounded leadership.

Chapter 4

HOW LEADERS LISTEN
Spiritual Discernment for Transformation

꧁ ꧂

Leadership is fraught with dangers. Half of managerial decisions fail.[12] What's a leader to do? Spiritual discernment, practiced by the leaders introduced in chapters 1–3, keeps a leader operating on all cylinders. This chapter explores the practice of spiritual discernment, essential to a spiritually grounded leader's toolbox.

Leadership is fraught with dangers. Leaders become lightning rods, recipients of people's often unrealistic expectations. People project their hopes and fears onto leaders and as a result, leaders and their actions become larger than life. In Western societies, leaders are expected to provide technical fixes for all kinds of problems, even those that have no technical fix. Many problems require wrestling with conflicting values among multiple stakeholders, and leaders who help their organizations do this work often meet resistance and become unpopular. Leaders bear the brunt of scapegoating. Occasionally they are even assassinated.[13]

Studies of senior managers' decisions show that half of the decisions made are no longer adhered to after two years.[14] Senior managers use the most successful decision-making practices least often and the least successful practices most often. Studies show that most managers can, in retrospect, identify their decision successes and failures, but they rarely subject them to systematic analysis, thus slipping into failure-prone decision-making practices time and again. These failure-prone practices include imposing decisions by edict or coercion, taking a problem-solving approach to decisions, and cutting off exploration of alternatives too soon. Successful practices include articulating objectives and asking employees to discover ways of meeting those objectives, and various forms of participative decision making. The successful practices encourage learning and innovation and most often result in decisions that prove beneficial to the organization over the long term. The failure-prone practices most often result in decisions that don't work, are costly in terms of dollars and/or reputation, and are eventually abandoned. Well-known decision failures include Disney's decision to locate EuroDisney near Paris, Ford's decision not to fix the Pinto's gas tank after its danger was discovered, and Nestlé's decision to continue to market infant formula in third-world countries.[15]

Most leaders want to make good decisions for their organizations, and their failed decisions are not for lack of trying. Because of such factors as time pressure, their perceived need to appear decisive, and unrealistic expectations from boards and employees, leaders often slip into decision-making practices that do not serve them well. Spiritual discernment can help leaders navigate through the dangers of leadership and can help them make decisions that will stand the test of time.

What is discernment? The Latin word *discernere*, "to separate" or "to distinguish" or "to sift through," is the origin of the English word "discernment." Discernment involves "sifting through" interior and exterior experiences to know which ones help one stay centered and which pull one away from centeredness.

Spiritual discernment is a process of going deeper. It is drawing on one's whole self, heart, mind, soul, and spirit. It includes and transcends intellectual analysis. It includes and transcends emotional intelligence. It is the bringing together of all of one's faculties within the larger context of the transcendent. In spiritual discernment, one learns to distinguish the real from the illusory, the wheat from the chaff. Through being deeply spiritually grounded, the discerner cuts through the usual distractions and attachments that obscure accurate perception, and seeks to see reality clearly.

Spiritual discernment is practiced both individually and corporately.[16] Even when done individually, it is never in isolation.

Individual and corporate discernment dance together, hand in hand. Corporate discernment requires prepared hearts and minds of the individuals involved. Individual discernment requires the support of a community, nurturing and grounding the person's spiritual life. Individual discernment also requires the accountability of a community, offering checks and balances to the individual's discernment.

HISTORICAL DEVELOPMENT

Although spiritual discernment, as a term, arose in the Christian tradition, the practice also appears in other spiritual traditions, referred to in different ways. The roots of the practice reach back as far as Aristotle. Aristotle outlined the components of decision making as finality and means. Finality, he maintained, is the ultimate goal of humans: the common good, personal virtue, and happiness. When people deliberate, they weigh different means of achieving this ultimate goal. Authentic deliberation involves always keeping finality in view and choosing means that are consistent with finality.[17]

The roots of discernment are also found in the Hebrew Scriptures and tradition. In the biblical worldview, Aristotle's "finality," the ultimate end of humans, translates into knowing the will of God and doing it. Such passages as

Speak, Lord, for your servant listens (1 Sam. 3:10)

O that my people would listen to me, that Israel would walk in my ways (Ps. 81:13)

Those who seek me diligently find me (Prov. 8:17)

reflect a worldview in which humans understand that knowing the will of God and doing it are both desirable and possible.

Early Christians blended Aristotle, the Hebrew Scriptures, and the New Testament as they began to articulate their understanding of spiritual discernment. Such New Testament passages as

He who has ears to hear let him hear (Matt. 13:43)

The one who belongs to God listens to the words of God (John 8:47)

> Let the person who has an ear listen to what the Spirit says to the churches (Rev. 2:7)

built on Old Testament passages that urged believers to listen to God and do God's will. The desert fathers and mothers developed teachings on discernment, which were later systematized by monks like John Cassian (d. 435) and John Climacus (d. 649). Ignatius of Loyola (d. 1556) wrote the first long treatise on discernment, which subsequently became the strongest influence on Christian discernment, though many other Christians, such as Carmelites and Quakers, also developed strong discernment traditions.

Analogues to the Christian discernment process also occur in other traditions. In the Buddhist tradition, the Buddha teaches "the importance of opening the eye of Dhamma, allowing one to see things just as they are."[18] According to the yogic traditions, past actions "cloud a person's ability to see the world clearly; the practices of yoga purify a person's karma, allowing one to see things as they are."[19] The Sioux tradition refers to the "eye of the Great Spirit" enlightening one's heart so that one might "see everything" and through this vision help one's neighbor.[20] In Sufi understanding, after initiation into the Sufi path the dervish continues the journey according to the principle of *La ilaha ilallah*, called the sword of light because of its power in dispelling illusion and revealing truth.[21]

Because discernment has been most fully articulated in the Christian tradition, this chapter provides an exposition of the practice in Christian language. At the same time, it is important to note that a similar exposition could be provided in the language of other traditions.

In Christian understanding, discernment occurs in the larger context of God's love. God's loving care envelops all, making no distinction between the secular and the sacred. Discernment is about hearing God's call in the midst of where one serves, whatever the context, knowing that God is active even in the midst of the messiest of situations. Hearing God's call and responding to God results in freedom, freedom from the need to please others, freedom from attachment to personal gain. As one hears God's voice in the midst of the cacophony of voices all around, both internal and external, one moves into ever greater freedom.

Over the years, Christians have articulated specific guidelines for practicing discernment: for preparation, for recognizing impediments to discernment, for the practice of discernment itself. Guidelines for preparation for discernment include nurturing a trusting attitude toward God, learning to listen, prayerfulness, familiarity with Scripture, humility, and patience.[22] Widely recognized impediments to discernment include self-interest, self-absorption, self-righteousness, desire for security, attachment to a particular outcome, and desire for certainty.[23] The discernment process itself requires maintaining an open and reflective attitude; an ability to listen to where God might be speaking, including through unexpected people and events; patience in waiting for God's answer; an ability to live with ambiguity; and a willingness to test the discernment by its fruits.

DISCERNMENT AND LEADERSHIP

How does all of this relate to leaders? Leaders face many pressures each day. A cacophony of voices surrounds them. They live in the midst of endless busyness and uncompleted to-do lists. People look to them for answers to complex problems for which the leaders lack adequate understanding and problem-solving skills.

As noted above, studies show that half of the decisions made in American companies fail. The primary causes of these failures are (1) premature commitments, (2) overemphasis on analytic evaluations, and (3) using failure-prone decision-making practices.[24] As Delbecq et al. point out in their article "Discernment and Strategic Decision Making,"[25] spiritual discernment can usefully be brought to bear on this problem, helping leaders address these common decision failures. This section examines each of the article's five principles for bringing discernment to decision making, illustrating each principle with examples from the leaders and organizations introduced in chapters 1–3.

1. Entering the Decision Process with a Reflective Inner Disposition

Foundational to bringing spiritual discernment to a decision, a reflective inner disposition must be cultivated. Far from being a template that can be pulled out of a bag of tricks at the moment it is needed, spiritual discernment grows out of ongoing inner preparation. While this inner preparation can take a wide variety of forms, it can be neglected only at the leader's peril.

For example, Bob Carlson's practices of walking in nature, listening to music, and attending worship services keep him nurtured and centered for his role as co-CEO at Reell Precision Manufacturing. When he doesn't get enough time for his spiritually renewing practices, Bob notices the difference:

> I think the big enemy of spirituality is busyness and the lack of reflective time, of quiet time. When things get really busy, when there's travel, board meetings, and shareholder meetings, and a number of things going on at the same time, I'll wake up some days and think, "You know, there's just not much happening right now in a spiritual sense."

Bob finds that his quiet, reflective time is essential to maintaining his depth and effectiveness as a leader.

In chapter 3 we observed Genny Nelson taking time to get away from the pressures of leadership at Sisters of the Road Café. Genny's journaling practice keeps her attentive, centered, and aware. Her time-outs to pray in special places in the neighborhood, such as in the downtown chapel, ground her and give her perspective on the challenges she faces. These practices cultivate a calm and open inner disposition, and they form the foundation for her ongoing dialogue with God, which she maintains throughout the day.

Theresa McCoy, former director of Greyston Family Support Services, maintained her regular practice of doing her chanting prayers. Even on busy days, she took the time to pray, whether at home or in the office. In addition, she noticed her reactions to people and stopped to reflect on them. As we saw in chapter 3, Theresa sought to step away from reactivity and into groundedness — for example, when she noticed her strong negative reaction to an opinionated person and, upon reflection, saw the same thing in herself. Theresa's practices formed her inner disposition and prepared her for discernment.

Theresa was supported in nurturing her predisposition for discernment by her organization. At Greyston Foundation, the umbrella organization under which Greyston Family Support Services lies, a process parallel to the Christian discernment process is articulated in Buddhist terminology. Bernie Glassman, the founder of Greyston, articulated a threefold sequence for perceiving reality: (1) not-knowing, or shedding preconceived notions; (2) bearing witness, or gazing steadily at what is; and (3) healing, or taking action that will lead to spiritual transformation. Greyston leaders practice this process and integrate it into their life in the organization.

2. Patience in the Discovery of the Underlying Nature of the Decision Issue

While leaders often face enormous pressures to make decisions quickly, premature decisions are the leading cause of decision failure.[26] This is primarily because leaders respond to the superficial presenting issue of a decision rather than taking the time to explore the underlying issues. A leader practicing spiritual discernment needs to exercise patience in allowing different viewpoints and underlying issues to surface.

Bob Carlson is a good example of a leader exercising patience in the face of diverse issues. As we saw in chapters 2 and 3, in the economic downturn of early 2001, Reell Precision Manufacturing faced a 30 percent drop in revenues. Some members of the senior leadership team favored layoffs and some favored salary reductions, with a 6-5 split in the then 11-member cabinet. While it would have been easy to push for a decision or call for a vote in order to ease the tension of the economic pressures, co-CEO Bob Carlson helped the team labor together and examine all of the issues. For example, while layoffs would ease the immediate budget crunch, what would be their impact on morale? How would each course of action further Reell's mission and square with its Direction Statement? The team finally agreed on salary reductions, knowing that, to the best of their ability, they had thoroughly examined the implications of both possible decisions.

3. Undertaking the Hard and Time-Consuming Work of Gathering Information

Leaders practicing discernment not only need patience in unearthing underlying issues, they also need to do the hard work of thorough information gathering. Too often decisions are short-circuited because leaders fail to ask what information is needed, or they fail to gather all the necessary information, or they fail to pursue the further relevant questions that arise once the information is gathered.

As Joe Clubb led the strategic planning process for St. Joseph's Hospital at HealthEast, he did the hard and time-consuming work of gathering information. He involved all the stakeholders and elicited their input. He talked with the Sisters of St. Joseph, whose forebears had founded the hospital in 1853, to hear their perspective on the mission, how it had been lived out over the years, and how they thought it should be lived out as HealthEast moved into the future. He gathered information from nurses about clinical issues and personnel issues. He gathered information from physicians about clinical issues. He gathered information from the board and administration about mission, financial issues, and how St. Joseph's fit into the larger structures and long-range plan at HealthEast. In all the information gathering, he sought to maintain an attitude of prayerful attentiveness, being open to all voices, and eliciting different points of view.

4. Reflection and Prayer

Dealing with underlying issues and processing vast amounts of information from multiple stakeholders are not easy tasks. Reflection and prayer help leaders sift through data and pay attention to what is most important. Discernment

> is not a promise of "technical" solutions, or secret knowledge that eliminates uncertainty or suffering from the process. Discernment rather gives us a sense we are proceeding in the right direction, and that "God is with us," sharing gifts of peace, love, and joy even in the difficult discovery process.[27]

Leaders who experience increased freedom and a sense of inner peace know that they are on the right track. A leader who experiences agitation, fear, or an uneasy feeling in the pit of her stomach knows to pay attention, knows that something could be amiss.

When Genny Nelson brought Sisters of the Road Café's financial struggles to God and said, "I'm laying it at your feet," she experienced God's peace and a fresh perspective on her struggles. She gained insight into steps she needed to take, and she knew she was on the right track.

U2 relies on all members of the band to exercise leadership and create the atmosphere in the band and the larger U2 community depicted in chapter 1. Because of the depth of trust and honesty in the group, everyone is expected to speak up when an issue needs to be addressed. As The Edge says, "When I feel uneasy with the direction we're going, I need to speak up and call the person or group on it." A band member pays attention to his feelings, to that uneasy sense he might get in the pit of his stomach, and he speaks his truth. This commitment to speaking truth to one another has saved band members from inflated egos taking over and has kept the band together for twenty-five years, highly unusual for a rock band.

5. Tentative Decisions and Attention to Outcomes

Successful discernment relies on the "contemplative pause" when the discernment nears its conclusion. Leaders ask themselves, "What does the fruit of this decision seem to be?" They apply the tried and true tests of discernment. Are the "fruits of the Spirit" (Gal. 5:22–23) — i.e., love, joy, peace, patience, kindness, generosity, faithfulness, gentleness, and self-control — more in evidence? Do the leader and other members of the organization feel an increased sense of freedom to live into their callings and to live out the organization's calling? Is morale higher? Have energy and creativity increased?

When Reell Precision Manufacturing's cabinet decided to take graduated salary cuts in 2001 rather than do layoffs, they paused to notice the implications before implementing the decision. Comparing their decision to past similar decisions in the company helped them anticipate the fruits of their discernment. And they continued to pay attention once they carried out the decision. Bob Carlson reported increased energy, increased morale, and an increased sense that "we're all in this together." Perhaps the most important confirmation Bob Carlson noted was from those who were initially skeptical:

> Several of the people who were for the layoffs have come back, twelve to eighteen months later, and said, "You know, I think the salary reductions were the right decision."

CONCLUSION

Leadership is fraught with peril. Pressure for quick decisions, the culture's overreliance on rational analysis, and the perceived need to appear decisive are but a few of the forces that can impair a leader's ability to make good decision. By practicing discernment, spiritually grounded leaders are less likely to fall prey to the dangers surrounding them. Maintaining a reflective inner disposition, patiently seeking underlying issues, gathering information, approaching a decision with reflection and prayer, and testing a decision by its fruits all help keep a leader operating on all cylinders.

PART TWO

And Back Out

INTRODUCTION

In part 1, we glimpsed soul at work in different settings, then moved behind the scenes to examine the leaders of those organizations, focusing on their inner lives and spiritual discernment practices.

Part 2 builds on the foundation of discernment to move back out into the life of the organization as a whole. With the grounding of discernment-based leadership, organizations can integrate their values and spirituality throughout their structures and processes. Spirituality can permeate the organization as a whole. While the stories and insights in this section are relevant to a wide range of organizations, from families to churches to businesses to nations, this book focuses on a subset of that range in order to consider in more depth manifestations of spirituality in related organizations. And while the organizations considered here have some things in common (they all need to stay afloat financially, they all need efficient and effective internal operations in order to achieve their organizational goals, they all compete with other providers of their products or services), they also exhibit certain differences. Businesses and nonprofits operate under different constraints and have different goals. Health-care organizations, sometimes run as businesses and sometimes as nonprofits, share certain aspects with each, and also have their own unique set of tasks and challenges. In order to be most practically useful to real people in real organizations, part 2 is divided into three types of organizations: business, health care, and nonprofits. Chapter 5 will considers the case of businesses where organizational spirituality is manifested as "double bottom lines" that include factors besides financial profit or direct shareholder value. Chapter 6 considers health-care organizations, where an attention to the organizational soul provides a context for the distinct but intertwined missions of healing and organizational sustainability. And chapter 7 looks at a number of nonprofits where noble purposes are amplified and sustained by an attention to organizational soul. Then chapter 8 considers the process of corporate discernment, just as chapter 4 examined individual discernment.

Part 1 provided glimpses into three businesses that are examined in more detail in part 2: Southwest Airlines, Greyston Bakery, and Reell Precision Manufacturing. Because Reell Precision Manufacturing figures prominently in chapter 8 and reappears in part 3, chapter 5 focus on other businesses, expanding the view of Southwest Airlines and Greyston Bakery offered in part 1, and adding Document Management Group of Dublin, Ireland. Likewise, chapter 6, on health care, picks up where part 1 left off with HealthEast, and adds discussions of Mercy Medical in Mason City, Iowa, and Our Lady's Hospice in Dublin. Chapter 7, on nonprofits, expands on part 1's Sisters of the Road Café and adds discussions of Sophia Housing in Dublin and the Shalem Institute in Washington, D.C.

Chapter 8 goes into more depth with the process of corporate discernment, used in various forms in the decision-making processes of many of the organizations examined in part 2. Just as individual discernment provides the foundation for the spiritually grounded leaders in part 1, so corporate discernment serves as a foundation for the spiritually grounded organizations in part 2. After a brief introduction to corporate discernment, chapter 8 focuses on three organizations in part 2 that use the process.

Chapter 5

BROADENING THE BALANCE

Honoring What Really Matters

🙢 ❧

SOUTHWEST AIRLINES

"Our number-one customer is our employee," claims Rita Bailey,[28] former director (Bailey retired in 2002) of the University for People at Southwest Airlines. For the first airline to define itself as a customer-service business, such a statement seems odd. How can putting the customer second result in the best customer service of any airline? Yet Southwest's philosophy — that if employees are treated well, they will in turn treat customers well — has paid off.

Southwest Airlines' story, a tribute to the indomitable human spirit, began in 1966 when Rollin King approached Herb Kelleher about starting an airline together and Herb responded, "Rollin, you're crazy. Let's do it!" A story of fighting for survival against impossible odds, Southwest's story illustrates how a culture which unleashes the human spirit can undergird a successful business model. Forged out of innovation in the face of adversity, Southwest's culture of encouraging creativity, joy, passion, teamwork, and esprit de corps proved to give it the competitive edge it needed in a cutthroat business environment. Once Southwest turned a profit for the first time in 1973, its leaders looked around and realized what a good thing they had going. By sustaining this culture, Southwest Airlines could capitalize on the human spirit in its fullest expression. They could harness the power of fun, love, and creativity for business success. They have done so, and have enjoyed a profit every year since 1973, an unheard-of record in the airline industry.

Thus, a culture was born. But how did they learn how to sustain it? Many a company had stories of passion, hard work, and esprit de corps during its founding years, only to lose those attributes when the company grew larger and became successful enough to lose its sense of urgency for survival.

Southwest was different. First, its leaders realized that its "soft" characteristics formed the foundation of its success, that they were not merely incidentals that could be ignored and allowed to wither away. Second, they discovered they could sustain that culture. By paying attention to what formed it in the first place, and by hiring and training for the same attributes, they could ensure their continued success.

Rita Bailey, during her tenure as director of the University for People, coined the acronym ACES to summarize Southwest's approach to sustaining the culture: attract, communicate, educate, and support. First, Southwest attracts the right people, hiring for attitude and only then training for skills, in contrast to the hiring practices of most businesses. As noted in chapter 1, Rita Bailey maintains that hiring fun people is how the airline gets people to do fun things. According to Bailey, training for skills is not difficult: "If they have the right attitude you can teach people pretty much anything, because if they have the right attitude they want to learn." On the other hand, "You can bring in somebody with all of the skills, and if they have a different attitude than what you want in the organization, you can't teach nice. You can teach behaviors that look like nice, but that doesn't make me nice."

Second, Southwest communicates expectations. In the interview process, in the orientation process, and in the training process, expectations are clarified repeatedly. This communication ensures that employees know that Southwest wants personal caring, a sense of servanthood, and a sense of customer service in its employees. Bailey remarks, "If you're a pilot, we want you to come out of the cockpit and talk to the customers as they're boarding; we don't want you to sit in there with the door shut."

Third, Southwest focuses on education. Obvious as it may sound, education at Southwest is about learning. "Most people have been taught how to be taught, not how to learn," remarks Bailey. That is, they attend class expecting information to be poured in, and then they immediately forget it when they're back on the job and the environment doesn't reinforce what they've been taught. At Southwest, learning occurs in a myriad of ways. Employees receive training in the classroom, which is then reinforced on the job; they are given access to the resources that will help them do their job effectively; and they receive training on both the technical and relational aspects of their jobs. For example, if an employee is learning how to give performance feedback as a supervisor, the emphasis is on the goal:

> What's the purpose of this and how would you like the person to feel? Are you doing this because the company says I have to fill out a performance appraisal every six months, or am I doing this because I really want this person to have everything they need to succeed?

Bailey claims that the latter approach ensures that "your chances for success, both technically and spiritually, are going to be a lot stronger."

Finally, the fourth letter of ACES represents the ongoing support that employees receive. For example, Southwest has the highest supervisor-to-customer-service-agent ratio of any airline, believing that supporting frontline employees is the most important factor for success. Coaching and mentoring occur through this emphasis on supervision, as well as through upper management walking around and making themselves available to middle managers. Furthermore, whenever there is a problem, upper management checks it out, seeking the root of the problem, being careful not to blame the frontline employee if the problem lies elsewhere: "[Evidence] often points to a leader who is for whatever reason not being effective," reports Bailey, who continues to explain that the leader would then be given the support needed to turn around and give effective support to the frontline employee.

Bailey is the first to admit that employees don't live up to Southwest's behavioral goals 100 percent of the time. The important thing is that when they don't, the organization as a whole is set up to help them change. During orientation, employees learn to support the Southwest culture when they encounter an employee who isn't displaying the appropriate attitude:

> I'm not going to tell you that out of thirty thousand people everybody was the cheerleader for the organization. We told people in the orientation, "You know what? There are going to be people out there who don't display the kind of behavior that we're talking about here. It's your responsibility not to fall prey to that but to help them make a turnaround. Help them find their light again."

What are the results of this relational culture? How does this culture affect such business issues as efficiency and budget cuts?

While some customer-service businesses address efficiency by, for example, telling customer-service agents they should spend only a certain number of minutes on the phone with each customer, and by reprimanding them if they go over their allotted time, Southwest takes a different approach. Southwest gives customer-service agents the big picture and then trusts them to do what's appropriate. Rita Bailey explains:

> We explained to them we want to accommodate as many customers as possible in a given day. So, that's not to say spend thirty minutes on the call with every customer, but use the appropriate amount of time. We trust your judgment and we want to make sure that we have served that customer and that we have created the experience that's going to bring them back.

The result? Calls are handled efficiently, and customers express how much they enjoy calling Southwest.

What about budget cuts? What happens when times get tough economically? For example, fuel cost increases affect the airline industry dramatically. When fuel costs spike, it's not unusual for employees to get a letter at home from the CEO, reports Bailey, saying something like:

> Hey, family, we are all in this together. Let me tell you why we need to cut $20 million off the budget. Fuel costs have spiked and for us a penny means a million dollars. We could do what most organizations do, we could lay off, we could cut parts of the operation, we could

increase the fares, but what we want to do first is we want to appeal to all of you as owners of this organization to contribute in any way that you can. If each of us saves just $5 a day, you multiply that times 30,000 people, that adds up.

Often the number would be exceeded, because some people would realize, "I can save twenty-five dollars a day, not just five dollars a day." Such things as not wasting materials, turning off computers, not calling in sick, adjusting schedules so that not as many employees are working on a day when the workload is lighter, all contributed to saving money. When everyone took responsibility for belt-tightening measures, more drastic measures could often be avoided.

As a result of its conservative growth and we're-all-in-this-together approach to financial squeezes, Southwest Airlines has never had to lay off employees, even after 9/11, when all other airlines did. Two locations were closed over Southwest's history, Denver and Beaumont, Texas. In those cases, employees were given plenty of notice and the opportunity to relocate. Similarly, more recently, with Internet sales increasing, three of Southwest's nine reservation centers were closed. Again, employees knew far in advance. Both with the location closures and reservation center closures, as much as possible was done through attrition, then people were encouraged to relocate, then people were offered early retirement packages, and finally, for those remaining, counselors were provided to help them find other jobs.

After 9/11, Southwest's relationship building paid off. Afraid to fly, customers called to cancel their reservations and said, "Southwest, you've been there for us and now we want to be there for you. You keep the money; we don't want the refund." Similarly, employees, knowing sales were down, wanted to give back. Southwest's leadership, afraid that people would give money they didn't have, limited the amount employees could give in payroll deductions, and still employees gave back over two million dollars. Senior executives did not take pay from September 11 until January, not deferring their pay but simply letting it go.

Interestingly, at Southwest the customer is not always right. "The customer is sometimes wrong. We don't carry those sorts of customers. We write to them and say, 'Fly somebody else. Don't abuse our people,'" Herb Kelleher was quoted as saying by Tom Peters in *Reader's Digest* in 1995.[29] For example, to a customer who had written numerous complaint letters to which employees had carefully responded, but who was still dissatisfied, Herb wrote, "Dear Mrs. Crabapple, We will miss you. Love, Herb."[30] *Reader's Digest* received a lot of affirming mail in response to its snippet about Southwest's policy.

How does all this work out from a business standpoint? As noted earlier, Southwest has made a profit every year since 1973, a period in which other airlines struggled to sustain even three or four consecutive years of profitability.[31] And contrary to a common misconception, Southwest is the most unionized airline in the industry, with 85 percent of employees in unions. Furthermore, Southwest has sustained a steady 10–15 percent growth rate since 1973. And Southwest's stock is currently worth more than that of all other major U.S. airlines combined.

At Southwest, leaders believe that people can have the best of both worlds, both business success and personal integrity and fulfillment. Bailey reflects on what she might ask herself after a lifelong career in business:

> If you were to die tomorrow, what would people say about you? What's your life been about? Has it been about making life miserable for the people who work for you because they didn't meet their quotas? Or has it been about helping people who needed help; you helped them grow, you helped them with an opportunity.

From Herb Kelleher's "Rollin, you're crazy. Let's do it!" in 1966 to today's wildly successful airline, Southwest Airlines has demonstrated that a business model based on unleashing the power of the human spirit works. By emphasizing fun, joy, love, passion, and esprit de corps, Southwest cultivates relational competence and business success.

GREYSTON BAKERY

Greyston Bakery, in many ways quite different from Southwest Airlines, also demonstrates how spirituality can be integrated throughout a business. A small business founded by Bernie Glassman in New York in 1982 (the forerunner to the Greyston Foundation, introduced in part 1), Greyston's Buddhist foundation defines its values. Convinced that for-profit businesses were the best way to revitalize the inner city, Bernie Glassman moved into Yonkers just as other businesses were moving out. He believed that "unemployable" people could become employable if given an opportunity, and Greyston Bakery became that opportunity. Glassman recalls,

> We were working with folks who were supposedly untrainable and unusable — and they created top-of-the-line products. That was what I was looking to do — to create things that were beautiful with folks who society felt couldn't do anything.[32]

Greyston continues to bake high-end cakes and tarts for some of New York's best restaurants. The bakery's products have also been served at the White House and at Lincoln Center. In addition, Greyston makes all the brownies for Ben and Jerry's Chocolate Fudge Brownie ice cream, as well as making products for four other Ben and Jerry's flavors. Glassman comments, "It was a Zen idea: to create a profit-making enterprise to support a spiritual and social goal."[33]

While built on Buddhist principles, Greyston welcomes people of all faiths and people of no faith. Greyston Bakery's current CEO, Julius Walls, once headed for the Roman Catholic priesthood and currently a Protestant preacher, now views the bakery as his ministry. Each day he starts his work day with this prayer,

> Lord Jesus, as I enter this workplace I bring your presence with me. I speak your peace, your grace, and your perfect order into the atmosphere of this space. I acknowledge your lordship over all that will be spoken, thought, decided, and accomplished within this day. Lord Jesus, I thank you for the gifts you have deposited in me and I do not take them lightly, but commit to using them responsibly and well. Give me a fresh supply of truth and beauty on which to draw as I do my job. Anoint my creativity, my ideas, and my energy so that even my

smallest task may bring you honor. Lord, when I am confused, guide me. When I am weary, energize me. Lord, when I am burnt out, infuse me with the light of the Holy Spirit. May the work that I do and the way that I do it bring hope, life, and courage to all that I come in contact with today and oh, Lord, in this day's most stressful moments may I rest in you. I pray this in the mighty, matchless, magnificent, and merciful name, in the name that is above all names, my Lord and Savior, Jesus Christ. Amen.

Formal expressions of Greyston Bakery's spiritual foundation include the moment of silence at meetings and the Way of Council. Every meeting opens with a moment of silence, a time to pause and be in touch with one's spiritual source. As CEO Walls explains it, "I tell people that they can do whatever they want during the moment of silence. I tell them that I pray, that others meditate, and that they can do whatever works for them." The moment of silence serves as a reminder that participants in a meeting, far from being independent individuals, instead are part of something much larger, are interdependent with one another and with the universe. Such a reminder helps participants let go of ego and prepare to search for the common good when they enter a meeting.

Bakery gatherings use the Way of Council, introduced in chapter 2 under Theresa McCoy's leadership, when they want to deepen their relationships with one another. Participants sit in a circle and pass around a talking piece, speaking only when they have the talking piece and leaving a respectful silence between speakers. They learn the same five practices outlined in chapter 2: listening from the heart, speaking from the heart, spontaneity, being of lean expression, and confidentiality. As these "unemployable" employees engage in the nitty-gritty of daily work in the bakery, they share their struggles with one another, and in the process they build strong relationships. They learn how to ask for and receive support. They gain not only external skills but also internal strength.

Greyston links community development to personal transformation. Both elements are important in the bakery as well as, of course, profitability. Greyston Bakery was one of the pioneers of the "double bottom line": rather than focusing solely on the financial bottom line, Greyston considers both profitability and personal/community development as equally important.

CEO Walls found himself drawn to Greyston because he identified with this double bottom line. First introduced to Greyston when he called on them while working for a chocolate company hoping to gain Greyston as a customer, he gradually learned what they were doing. "These were my people," he recalls. "Frankly, I saw something that surprised me: people of color working in the bakery, in the office. I wanted to join this organization and work with my people." He relates his own story:

> I grew up in the projects, and most of my friends or neighbors didn't think they had much choice. If you were going to earn money in my community, more than likely you were going to do it through drug dealing or some other illegal means. There were not black businessmen in my community. There were not opportunities for jobs for black males in my community.

The turning point came for Walls when his parish priest paid his tuition so that he could attend a private Catholic high school. He felt drawn to Greyston because it provided an opportunity for him to give back. He uses Jesus' parable of the sower to describe his journey and his work at Greyston:

> The sower is throwing out seeds, and the first set of seeds is eaten by birds, the second set falls on stones and they sprout up but their roots can't grab anything so they die, others fall among thorns and so they start to grow but eventually the thorns choke them out. Some fall on good ground and they are able to place their roots down and take hold and grow. When I think of the people that I grew up with, some were eaten by birds, killed; some had fallen on stone, they didn't have any resources available to them in their lives; some had fallen among thorns, they succumbed to some obstacle that prevented them from growing. At Greyston I was fortunate enough to fall on good ground. What I am hoping to do is to create more fertile ground for other people to grow.

Julius's hope is being fulfilled. Greyston Bakery has become a role model for socially conscious businesses. Its profits support Greyston Housing, Greyston AIDS health center, Greyston child care, and

Greyston technology center. Balancing the double bottom line proves challenging at times, as the bakery seeks to attain both success as a business and high standards of service to the community. The bakery's "Guiding Principles" help it chart its course:

> A portion of the Bakery's net profits will support the various nonprofit projects of the [Greyston] Foundation, the bakery's sole shareholder. The amount will be balanced against the need to reinvest in the business to remain competitive and the need to maintain a certain level of available working capital at all times.[34]

Furthermore, Greyston Bakery takes its double bottom line seriously, monitoring its progress toward nonfinancial goals just as carefully as it monitors its progress toward financial goals. Among other things, the bakery commits itself to "rigorously measure, document, ... and monitor the success of its open-hiring policy, skill building efforts, and employee turnover."[35]

Greyston Bakery's open-hiring policy means that it hires its employees first-come, first-served. That is, whenever Greyston announces a hiring day, it takes the first applicants in line until it has filled its available positions. New employees begin with an apprenticeship period, during which they receive five dollars an hour. It's not unusual for Greyston to hire people who are homeless, just out of prison, or just out of drug treatment programs. Approximately half of all apprentices persevere through the training period. Then employees can earn good wages and benefits, including regular wage increases based on time of service and performance. Furthermore, employees gain marketable skills, which they can transfer to other jobs. For example, Greyston has sent employees to train at the American Institute of Baking in Manhattan, Kansas.

The bakery promotes from within whenever possible, promoting entry-level workers to such positions as supervisor and manager. Of the fifty-five employees now at Greyston Bakery, fifty started in entry-level positions. Rodney Johnson, a former drug dealer who started at Greyston as an apprentice on the brownie line, has now worked his way up to production manager and was featured on CBS-TV's *60*

Minutes in January 2004. Wendy Powell, a homeless single mother, discovered Greyston and, over the course of nine years, received promotions from apprentice to bookkeeper to Walls's executive assistant.[36] Steve Gill came to Greyston after six years of incarceration, starting as an apprentice making brownies. He completed a college degree while working at Greyston and now has been promoted to chief purchasing clerk.[37]

The bakery seeks to balance remaining competitive in a market economy with treating its employees well. To that end, the bakery commits itself to

> pay employees fair wages for their skills. While for some employees this salary may not constitute a "living wage," the bakery is committed to working with these individuals to improve their financial self-sufficiency. To this end, the bakery will work with employees to increase their earning power by assisting them in improving their job readiness and baking skills. The bakery will encourage and support employees who seek outside vocational training, academic advancement, and professional non-bakery-related enrichment. The bakery will also support employees who seek greater self-sufficiency through employment elsewhere.[38]

Furthermore, Greyston Bakery firmly believes that its real-world environment serves as a better job-training ground than an artificial environment would. The bakery keeps up with technological advances in the industry, including automation:

> In order to maintain a profit and to assure that bakery employees are developing skills valuable in the modern marketplace, the bakery will automate its production when fiscally appropriate. The bakery management will monitor applicable technological trends in the baking industry in order to inform automation decisions. The bakery will strive to maintain and increase employment levels despite increased automation, through improved marketing efforts and sales growth.[39]

Now a $5 million business, Greyston Bakery is succeeding on the business front as well as on the social front. In March 2004 the bakery moved into a newly constructed $9.7 million building designed by architect Maya Lin, tripling its production area, and it views the years ahead as a time of expansion and greater vision. Julius Walls offers a baking analogy to illustrate Greyston's recipe for success:

> Any successful recipe has flour, sugar, eggs, and butter, because all of those ingredients are necessary to make the product work, but you also need time and temperature. Time to let the products bake and temperature to be applied to change the chemical nature of those products. The part of the analogy that I love most is that if you put the batter inside the pan it is at one level, but when you let the time and temperature take place it rises. That is what happens at Greyston. We put together all the ingredients. We mix them up and we apply some time and some heat and sometimes that heat is comforting and sometimes that heat burns, but it is always necessary for things to grow.

Walls adds, "I hope to always be part of a good recipe."

Document Management Group

Named one of the five best companies to work for in Ireland in 2003 and 2004, Document Management Group, made up of FileStores, Shred-It, and two other business-to-business services, grew out of a business which has been operating in Dublin for three decades. A family business focused on high-quality service, DMG has grown to 130 employees since its inception, expanding steadily since its founding — 30 percent each year for the past five years.

Tom Hefferon, managing director, cofounded the business and articulated the current vision statement:

> Our vision is to build a new business model, profitable and productive, where our people can find meaning, significance and success through their work, and where personal and workplace values align to achieve greater outward harmony and inner spiritual life. By this we will remain one of Ireland's Best Companies to work for while striving to become one of Ireland's top-ten "business to business" service providers, and "most admired" companies, as voted by our peers in the business community, with a reputation for "getting things done."

Motivated by his Catholic faith and at the same time seeking to be inclusive of all, Hefferon attempts to integrate spirituality and values throughout the company. He believes that, ultimately, only the spirituality- and values-based companies will survive:

> Spirituality in the workplace has huge potential; I think it has a significant future. In years to come, this could be in two centuries' time, I don't know, people will look back and say, "They just closed down companies that didn't do that."

Hefferon, aware of the pitfalls family businesses face, belongs to an international family business network. The network recognizes that family businesses tend to run into conflicts between "soft" family values and "hard" business values, and it helps businesses integrate the two. Hefferon uses the image of a clutch in a machine:

> You stand in the middle between the hard company values and the soft family values and you say, "We need to design a clutch for this machine," so they can meet and harness each other, so they can drive, rather than grind and break.

Half of the "clutch" Hefferon has designed is a written constitution that was presided over by all the family members, designating the family as a shareholder group: "We want them to say, 'Hold on, where is my dividend?' and thus think like business owners," claims Hefferon. This part of the clutch helps the family members recognize and value the hard business values.

The other half of the clutch helps harness the power of the soft values for the business and consists of such initiatives as the Excellence through People program and the Best Companies initiative. The Excellence through People program, started at FileStores in 2000, has focused on values, communication and involvement, and training. Like Southwest Airlines, FileStores wanted to harness the power of relational competence. Because the company had grown so much from the small family business it had been merely a few years before, the sense of being a close-knit family had faded. First, the Excellence through People program began with employees articulating their values, naming what was most important to them that they wanted to bring to work with them instead of parking it outside the door. Then the composite list of employee values became the value statement of the company, posted on the wall:

VALUE STATEMENT

Integrity

We will be open and honest with each other and our customers. We will earn trust through honesty, dignity, integrity and accuracy.

Pride

We will take pride in the excellent work we do. Our service will be dedicated to accuracy and efficiency, with reliability and flexibility. We will listen to our customers so that we can better meet their needs.

Harmony

Harmony, happiness and humour are three essentials for a good working environment. We commit to a special spirit of cooperation in working together, happy to serve the needs of our customers, as well as the work needs of each other.

Second, communication and involvement were stressed. How could employees know that they were part of something bigger, something of which they could be proud? The company worked on articulating a common purpose and on team building. Furthermore, participants created structures and processes for sustaining communication and involvement. For example, every employee now has the opportunity to meet individually with the managing director quarterly. Also, "information evenings" became routine: every six weeks the management updates staff on successes to celebrate and any issues the company faces, inviting employee input, and then following the event with a social evening.

Third, the group focused on training. How could new hires receive the training they needed to be successful, and how could employees continue to receive effective training as their jobs changed or they took on new responsibilities? The result was a training policy that articulated a commitment, "FileStores is fully committed to the continuous development of all employees through individually designed training programmes," and a two-pronged approach to carrying out the commitment. First, Colm Hefferon, training and quality manager, discusses with each of the department heads their goals for their departments. Second, he has conversations with individual staff in the departments, asking what kind of training they would like to receive. Then he designs a training program responsive to the needs of both groups, adjusting it as needed as the training proceeds. In response to the rapid growth in the company, the training department is currently creating a matrix that identifies the skills required for each job in the company and how training for each job should occur.

Hiring and induction also play an important role at DMG. DMG has identified seven signs that will indicate when the company has attained its vision. The first and most important sign, "Leaders who devote significant time and effort to recruiting and developing those around them," grew out of trial and error. Now, along with a thorough interview, applicants take a detailed psychometric test. Though expensive to administer, the test has proven worth its weight in gold in determining how well a potential employee will fit with the company's culture. As a simple example, Hefferon notes, "Somebody who has a high manageability index (meaning he likes to be managed closely) probably wouldn't fit in here, because we don't manage closely." Hefferon and the general manager must approve all new hires. After being hired, everyone goes through an induction process that includes a general orientation, an introduction to the company's values and standards, and health and safety information. Employees then receive ongoing support to help them attain and sustain the company's standards of service.

The list of seven signs also includes these indicators: "leaders who are surrounded by people willing to challenge their thinking," "clear and accountable decision-making and communication," "clear roles and responsibilities which support, inform and enable our people to do their job well," "business plans which are clear, communicated and accountable," "performance measures which are understood and which clearly align with our business plans," and "service excellence which is second to none; *doing what we do* is second nature to breathing."

In 2004, DMG started a Best Companies initiative, building on the success of the Excellence through People program. The Best Companies initiative focuses on those things that make DMG one of the best companies to work for. A current practice, such as promoting from within, maternity and paternity leave, support for education, job sculpting, or flextime, is highlighted each month. In addition, employees are invited to make suggestions that will improve their experience at the company. The goal of the Best Companies initiative is quality, both within and without.

Quality is important at DMG, since the company relies on employees to "go the extra mile" with customers. For example, if a customer calls FileStores wanting a file, he may not ask for it by the same name or subject he (or someone else in his company) gave when his company first transferred the file to FileStores. If a FileStores employee checks the database and can't find the entry, she might say, "I'm sorry, we don't have the John Doe file." If instead, she probes more deeply, perhaps asking, "Is that John Doe file you wanted a property surveillance file or a litigation file?" the caller might be able to identify it in another way. DMG wants its employees to act as detectives with customers, and is prepared to give them all the support they need, both technical and attitudinal, to help them do their best. As Tom Hefferon puts it,

> If we want [employees] to go the extra mile we must go the extra mile with them, and must create an atmosphere where they feel that we care for them and therefore that they care for what they do.

The purpose of the Best Companies initiative is to create that atmosphere. Hefferon believes that the practices that make DMG one of the Best Companies to work for also strengthen the business. For example, regarding maternity leave, Hefferon points out how the conventional wisdom in some companies is that you can't hire a female senior manager because she might get pregnant. At DMG, three of the six senior managers are women, and, in Hefferon's view, "Women who get far enough to apply to senior management situations have to be better in order to make it through the glass ceiling, so why not hire from that pool?" Realizing that the need for maternity leave doesn't arise very often, Hefferon believes that offering maternity leave is a good investment for the business.

Pleasantly surprised that DMG was named a Best Company to work for again in 2004, Hefferon outlined both the Best Company selection process and the rocky road DMG had traveled in 2003. In the selection process, two-thirds of the rating a company receives comes from that company's employees, who fill out extensive anonymous questionnaires. The remaining one-third comes from external auditors. In 2003, FileStores had been named the Fifth Best Company to work for in Ireland. Subsequently, FileStores and Shred-It merged, resulting in significant upheaval, including redundancy in ten positions. With the decision to merge, Hefferon reported that top management thought, "There goes our best company rating," but they realized they needed to merge in order to do what was best for the business. Management tried to do their best to soften the blow (although everyone in the redundant positions had relatively short terms of service, ranging from one to three years, all received generous severance packages), but the process was still difficult. When it came time to decide whether to enter the Best Company process for 2004, top management considered entering just FileStores rather than the merged company, DMG. But Hefferon, convinced that the only way to get information about how things were going was to take the risk, decided to enter as DMG. To his surprise, DMG received the Fifth Best Company award. Representative of how DMG employees feel about the company, Health and Safety Officer Mike Naidoo muses,

> I don't think the directors went out intentionally to set these standards. I think it's in them. They didn't come out here and say, "Oh my God, we have to treat everyone right today." It's just in them because they are that type of people.

Aware of both the strengths and limitations of being a family business, Tom Hefferon readily acknowledges his struggles and stands ever vigilant to nip problems in the bud. He also uses humor, playing off the culture of family. When DMG recently made its first major acquisition, a company in Northern Ireland, Hefferon announced the acquisition by sending out a birth announcement to the company, announcing the birth of a daughter to the company. Introducing the personnel who would be moving to the new office, he remarked that the marketing director would be buying some nice new dresses for the baby, that the manager would be changing her diapers, and that the accountant would be minding her piggy bank.

DMG, then, lives its spirituality and values throughout the organization. A flagship company for Tom Hefferon's vision of the future when all companies will have realized they need to evolve toward this vision in order to survive, DMG incarnates what it believes. Perhaps Mike Naidoo's suggestion can one day become a reality:

> If any companies wanted to see how to run a successful company, they should send someone here. Ask for permission for a week to work with us and then take that back to the owner of the place. That is one of the major pluses that we can offer.

CONCLUSION

Southwest Airlines, Greyston Bakery, and Document Management Group, though worlds apart in location and products, all demonstrate that spirituality and business, far from being irreconcilable foes, are natural partners. Through harnessing the creativity, passion, joy, and love of the human spirit, with or without a connection to religion, employees (even the hard to employ) can thrive, and businesses can succeed.

Chapter 6

Nurturing the Nurturers
Caring for the Whole Organization

❦

HealthEast

"The people value and respect me, listen to me and help me grow as a person and as a nurse. It's the people. That's why I work at HealthEast," wrote a nurse when HealthEast won the Best Minnesota Hospital Workplace award for 2003. The award, given by the Minnesota Hospital Association, honors hospitals that "go the extra mile" in enhancing employee satisfaction and retention. HealthEast won the award based on such factors as decrease in employee turnover and increase in employee engagement. HealthEast, like Southwest Airlines, focuses on relational competence, believing that "our employees are our number one asset."[40]

Mission

HealthEast, introduced in part 1, grew out of a merger of Baptist, Lutheran, and Catholic hospitals on the east side of the Twin Cities in Minnesota. Now a four-hospital, eleven-clinic health-care system, HealthEast boasted 7,600 employees serving 33,000 inpatients and 313,000 outpatients in 2004. Recognizing a common factor in their Christian heritage, the hospitals coming together articulated their joint mission, vision, goal, and values thus:

Mission

Rooted in Judeo-Christian values, our mission is high quality, compassionate, cost effective health care for the communities we serve.

Vision

Creating the best health care experience through a passion for caring and service.

Goal

We are the first choice for customers, physicians and employees.

Values

Life: Life is a gift to be valued highly.

Compassion: Caring attends to physical, emotional and spiritual dimensions of persons.

Respect: Each person is unique and deserving of respect.

Community: We exist to serve our community.

HealthEast integrates spirituality throughout its system, starting at the top. The vice president of spiritual care sits on the senior leadership team and has a voice in all deliberations. The Mission Committee sees to it that the mission is lived out throughout the organization. Directors' and other leadership meetings are usually opened with prayer. An endowed annual lecture, the Hultkranz lecture, provides physicians and leaders with speakers who address topics that integrate the disciplines of medicine, spirituality, and healing. In 2004, HealthEast did a major inquiry into the importance and validity of publicly stating and promoting its spiritual philosophy, as some had questioned whether HealthEast's Christian heritage was excluding people of other (or no) spiritual traditions. The result of the inquiry (where seven thousand employees were surveyed with a greater than 60 percent response rate) was a renewed commitment to its identity as a faith-based organization. HealthEast seeks to live out its Christian heritage while respecting other faith traditions, as articulated in its faith-based philosophy: "By sustaining HealthEast's Christian heritage and identity, we provide compassionate service that respects the dignity of each person and welcomes all faith traditions, cultures and communities."

HealthEast's culture puts relationships first. As we saw in chapter 1, Etta Erickson, program director for the cancer program, underscores the compassion and love and emphasis on relationships she experiences at HealthEast, contrasting that with other health-care organizations with which she is familiar.

A prime example of putting relationships first, Barb McIntyre has built relationships on her nursing teams at HealthEast for more than twenty-five years. She passes on to her staff the respect and support she receives from her superiors. She leads with a light touch, recognizing the pressure of her nurses' jobs. She communicates her care for each one as a person, doing things like expressing appreciation frequently and also sending annual Christmas cards in which she expresses gratitude for specific ways each has served in the previous year. She finds her employees coming to her to talk when crises arise in their personal lives. A few years ago the CEO took Barb to lunch, asking what HealthEast could learn from her about putting people first. Her retention and continuous improvement record had caught his attention, and he knew that she was incarnating HealthEast's values. Now Barb is held up as a role model, and she teaches others how to put people first, as she does.

For the past five years, HealthEast has adopted and adapted Interdisciplinary Clinical Practice (ICP), a program based in Grand Rapids and designed by Bonnie Wesorick,[41] as a way of systematically implementing its mission throughout the institution.

Interdisciplinary Clinical Practice

HealthEast's Interdisciplinary Clinical Practice program, introduced in chapter 2 under Joe Clubb's leadership, focuses on creating "a healthy work environment where patient-centered care will flourish."[42] Adopted at HealthEast in 1999 and soon thereafter adapted to HealthEast's particular needs, ICP seeks to create a "culture of shared partnership." ICP, designed to take a systems approach to health care, builds interdisciplinary partnerships.

More than thirty interdisciplinary partnership councils form the backbone of ICP at HealthEast. The partnership council is a "formal structure designed to develop and enhance partnering relationships of all disciplines in order to achieve a shared mission and vision."[43]

Eight to twelve employees from a variety of functions constitute a partnership council. For example, a nursing unit might have a partnership council consisting of a nurse, a housekeeper, a social worker, a manager, a chaplain, a physician, a pharmacist, a dietitian, and an educator, all of whom work on that nursing unit. Partnership councils meet monthly for two hours, seeking to engage the creative thinking of all members in order to elicit the group's collective wisdom. The meetings follow strict ground rules such as confidentiality, beginning and ending on time, suspending certainty and judgment, no domination, equal voice for all participants, and allowing multiple perspectives to surface prior to consensus. Two co-facilitators (neither of whom is the unit manager) chair the meeting, beginning with a brief check-in time in which participants share something from their lives — for example, a surprising moment they experienced during the past week between themselves and a patient. Next, someone briefly shares a patient story, serving to remind the group of its collective work. A patient story may include such elements as something unique about the patient, what the council member learned about the patient that allowed for effective individualized care, and how HealthEast responded well to the patient's needs. After the patient story, the council moves into the substance of its meeting: dialogue and consensus. Topics considered always come from staff, not administration. Since neither of the co-facilitators is a manager and since the group commits itself to allowing multiple perspectives to surface prior to consensus, a sense of safety pervades the group. At the first meeting and occasionally thereafter, the facilitators remind participants of the group's definitions of dialogue and consensus, contrasting dialogue with discussion and consensus with other forms of decision making. Once the group achieves consensus, the facilitators summarize the meeting's highlights and action items, to be posted on the unit's bulletin board. The meeting concludes with a brief checkout time, in which facilitators summarize the response of the group to the question, "What did we do today to positively impact patient care and the work environment?" The group then applauds the meeting's accomplishments and sets the next meeting time.

The ICP steering committee serves as a resource for all the partnership councils. The ICP system director and representatives from the various partnership councils comprise the steering committee, which also provides direction and planning for ICP, and evaluates its effectiveness. Steering committee members view themselves as "ambassadors" between partnership councils and corporate management. They seek to model the systems thinking of the ICP model, and they coach the conceptual shift from "individual thinking to group thinking and from bureaucratic management to collective stewardship for health care delivery."[44]

HealthEast has formulated a clear implementation plan for ICP. For example, the key goals for fiscal year 2003 included increasing awareness of the ICP initiative throughout the HealthEast staff, increasing grassroots and multidisciplinary participation in partnership councils, increasing manager/director engagement in partnership councils, and improving overall productivity and effectiveness of partnership councils. These visionary goals were then broken down into simple steps employees could take. For example, the "Improve overall productivity and effectiveness of HealthEast partnership councils" goal included such steps as "document improvements in patient care related to the recommendations and actions of respective partnership councils," "laminate and post the agreed upon key goals and ground rules for each partnership council at its site, i.e., partnership council meeting room and/or patient care area bulletin board," and "highlight resources available to partnership council co-chairs at quarterly co-chair workshop."[45]

ICP leaders carefully measure progress toward their goals, even going so far as to include specific measurement in their goals when appropriate. For example, the "Patient Satisfaction" goal for 2003 was to improve the Emotional Support Dimension of care given to each inpatient at HealthEast's four hospitals. Using carefully calibrated surveys, the Picker Institute Patient Satisfaction survey and the Press Ganey Patient Satisfaction survey, HealthEast wanted to improve the relevant responses by 2.5 percent. The "Healthy work environment" goal for fiscal year 2003 included the measurement

"Response to Question 6 of Partnership Council Survey (Co-Creating Healthy Work Cultures) designed to measure member engagement will improve by 2.5 percent." (Question 6 reads: "The organization enhances partnership within and across roles, departments, and disciplines." Employees answer "Yes" or "No" to the question.)

According to employees, the partnership councils have accomplished a number of things in the "healthy work environment" area, including improved teamwork, identification of role conflicts and conflict resolution, influence in staffing mix design, growth in mutual leadership, shared stress reduction ideas, improvement in morale, and an effective buddy system for new hires. With respect to patient care, the partnership council accomplishments include establishing a message board in the family waiting room, reducing multiple blood draws from the same patient, shortening turnaround time for urgent medications from the pharmacy to the patient, and computerized patient family education for oncology patients.

As noted in chapter 1, one of the goals of ICP is to improve the outcomes of "Moments of Truth." A Moment of Truth, as defined in the ICP glossary is

> Anytime a customer comes in contact with any aspect of an organization and has the opportunity to form an impression of the quality of that organization's service. HealthEast considers a Moment of Truth a [possible] Moment of Compassion.[46]

Holding in their awareness the possibility of each Moment of Truth being a Moment of Compassion, HealthEast employees build community and help one another live into HealthEast's "passion for caring and service."

Rituals and Celebrations

HealthEast also uses rituals and celebrations to keep its mission and vision front and center. For example, April is mission month. Employees reflect on their own sense of mission, both personally and professionally, and how their mission fits with HealthEast's mission. Through inspirational speakers, service projects, and the annual president's prayer breakfast, mission month serves as a time to celebrate successes and recommit to HealthEast's mission, both individually and as an organization.

A variety of worship services also serve to undergird HealthEast's mission and culture. In addition to special observances for Christmas, Easter, Lent, and other holidays, masses and other services are offered for family members of employees who have died. Chaplains serve not only patients but also employees, taking care to go beyond the Christian borders of HealthEast's foundation and meet people on their own ground.

One ritual created by the oncology leaders' partnership council is their annual overnight retreat. Designed to nurture the whole person of the oncology leaders, just as the oncology leaders nurture the whole person of each of their employees and patients, the retreat focuses on strategic planning, spiritual nurture, and social interaction. For example, one year Etta Erickson and Phyllis Novitskie planned the meditation time to include music, a setting in nature, and then a meditation on hands. The meditation included how each person's hands were formed, how their little hands were taught by their parents, how the hands came to serve, and how their hands connected them with one another. Concluding with a blessing on hands, Phyllis and Etta offered four words that exemplified each person and her gifts. After closing with music, the group went outside and ended the retreat with social time, building a bonfire, hitting golf balls, and telling funny stories. Etta reports,

> I think that relationship building outside of work is just crucial in terms of supporting the difficult times that come. There is a learning curve of experiencing it and then the value of it washing back over you. So when you go back the second time, and the third time, you say, "Ah, this is why we do this."

Thus, HealthEast puts into operation "passion for caring and service" and its explicit commitment to spirituality in the workplace in a variety of ways: through ICP, through mission month, through rituals, through celebrations, through retreats. By staying attentive to relationships and mission, HealthEast maximizes opportunities for Moments of Truth to become Moments of Compassion.

Mercy Medical

"Whatever you're doing around here is working because people sure smile and are helpful to me and my wife," glowed the Iowa farmer who walked into Mercy Medical's public relations office, unsolicited, to express his gratitude. Such expressions are not surprising at Mercy Medical–North Iowa, where excellence stands as the highest value.

Mission

St. Joseph Mercy Hospital, founded in Mason City by the Sisters of Mercy in 1916, is now known as Mercy Medical Center–North Iowa. Today the hospital and network sites boast over 2,760 employees and over 12,359 inpatient admissions. In the spirit of Catherine McAuley, who opened the first House of Mercy in Dublin in 1827, Mercy Medical Center (a branch of Trinity Health) articulates its mission as follows:

> We serve together in Trinity Health, in the spirit of the Gospel, to heal body, mind, and spirit, to improve the health of our communities, and to steward the resources entrusted to us.

Mercy Medical's core spirituality manifests itself throughout the system, starting at the top. Mercy's mission statement stands front and center in the organization, and Mercy's senior leadership hold themselves to high standards in being the first to live it out. The mission leader, whose primary responsibility is the integration of the mission throughout the system, sits on the senior leadership team, raising questions of faithfulness to the mission in every deliberation. In addition, all members of senior leadership are expected to model the mission, and their performance objectives include mission objectives.

How was this atmosphere created? And how is it sustained at all levels of the organization? It is both taught and caught.

First, Mercy emphasizes its roots. The story of founder Catherine McAuley continues to inspire leaders throughout the organization. McAuley's concern for the poor and underserved, especially women and children, as well as her concern for the whole person, continue to guide Mercy Medical today. Through presentations, workshops, and written materials, Mercy leaders learn about Mercy's roots and think together about how the founding charism can best be kept alive and appropriated today.

Second, the corporate mission office provides material to leaders, either in the form of a didactic leadership training series for new leaders, or in the form of published materials outlining Mercy's mission and values. Third, Mercy offers regular fall and spring conferences for employees, at which mission is emphasized. The annual re-missioning process reminds everyone of the importance of mission and the importance of conscious recommitment to it.

While being taught is very important, even more important, Mercy's core spirituality is caught. In the transition to lay leadership, many speak of the Sisters of Mercy modeling the spirituality and values, and making themselves available. Brandt Lippert, former vice president of human resources, for example, explains the impact the Sisters have had on him, despite their declining numbers. In describing their modeling and availability, he relates:

> They have done a nice job of schooling the leaders. If I personally had to point to someone, I'd point to Sister Marcia, who was here when I came in '78 and is still here. She is someone I feel very comfortable sharing concerns or issues with; she has been a touch point for me.

In like manner, Doug Morse, senior vice president of network and clinic management, speaks of learning "by ear." He also uses the image of a magnetic field: "I think the spiritual core is a very strong magnet for a lot of folks, and it keeps them here." In describing how people absorb the atmosphere, he gives a hypothetical example:

> I'm a new person. I've moved in from Timbuktu to be the medical records director. And I'll hear everything in orientation. But it will be over time when I see it lived out and then pass it on myself that I'll really get it.

Celebrations and Recognitions

Celebrations and recognitions start small and go up the chain. From the day-to-day recognitions of "Pat on the Back" and "Winning Ways" to the annual or biennial Mercy Legends, celebrations and recognitions are an integral part of Mercy Medical. The Pat on the Back award recognizes a day-to-day act of modeling of Mercy's values. Winning Ways recognizes suggestions employees make that advance Mercy's strategic initiatives, and recipients receive a small *W* to wear on their nametags.

The Wall of Excellence, created by a Human Resources team, grew out of the team's recognition that, as an organization, Mercy needed to celebrate the wonderful things occurring in its midst. Acknowledging the tendency of high achievers to be their own worst critics, the team wanted to shift the culture away from a perfectionist deficiency model to a positive celebratory model. As Brandt Lippert put it:

> If I'm told that I'm doing some really special things, what are the odds of my wanting to do more special things in the future? I mean, it's just one of those "duhs." And the Wall of Excellence is simply a way to be able to communicate that to a wider audience.

The three Golden Awards recognize physicians. Given quarterly, these awards are also posted on the Wall of Excellence. The Golden Heart award recognizes exceptional customer service, including bedside manner, compassion, and timely response. The Golden Hands award recognizes exceptional contributions to Mercy, including mentoring others, committee/task force participation, community service, and referrals to Mercy. The Golden Stethoscope award recognizes exceptional practice of healing, including approachability, coordination of patient care, patient/family involvement, and holistic care.

At monthly leadership staff meetings someone is always invited in to be honored for going beyond the call of duty, and his or her story is told. Likewise, at board of trustees' meetings, after the opening reflection, the same thing occurs. After the story is told, the board gives the person a standing ovation. As board member Corita Heid says, "Some of them are so touching there is not a dry eye in the room."

The Mercy Legend award, bestowed every year or two, recognizes that there are others, in addition to founder Catherine McAuley, destined to become legends for the institution. With a more formal process than the other awards, including letters of support, interviews, and numerical ratings according to specific criteria, the Mercy

Legends are chosen carefully. Surprised at the annual awards banquet with the award, Mercy Legend recipients often are deeply moved by the honor. Furthermore, as Brandt Lippert notes,

> The amazing thing is that the teams involved in the selection process are just as emotionally invigorated by the whole thing as the people who are getting the awards.

The annual awards banquet is merely one of a number of special events held throughout the year at Mercy. Like the awards banquet, the special events are often celebrations tied to recognitions or re-membrances. Special masses are offered in memory of employees or employee family members who have died. The annual holiday party might include a time of remembrance of those who have died in the past year. Special religious services are held during Christmas, Lent, and Easter.

Kailo: Support for Mercy's Employees

While the foregoing initiatives focus on the outward mission of Mercy Medical, the Kailo program focuses on helping Mercy live its mission internally. Launched in 1998 by three dynamic women, the Kailo program (Kailo is an Indo-European word meaning to be "whole") started with the awareness that caregivers often don't take care of themselves.

Determined to promote individual and organizational well-being by responding to felt needs, the Kailo team began by listening to their "customers," Mercy Medical's employees. The results surprised them. Instead of saying, "I'd like to lose weight, get more exercise, lower my cholesterol," as the team expected, employees surveyed replied, "I'm fatigued, depressed, anxious, in a violent relationship." Consequently the Kailo program, unlike traditional wellness programs that focus on medical risk indicators, has focused on sleep, depression, and abuse. Furthermore, respondents said, "We're busy and overstressed. This has to be on your time, not our time." The Kailo team requested that Mercy's administration take a leap of faith in its program by funding it on company time, and the administration agreed.

Also unlike traditional wellness programs, which deem March as diabetes month, April as heart disease month, May as hypertension month, the Kailo program has focused on one theme per year. For example, 2000's theme was sleep. As Laura McKibbin relates,

> We try to remind ourselves, "At the end of the year, what do we want employees to be able to say we did?" And if all they can say is, "Well, it's good to get sleep," we think that's great because we think people are bombarded by a billion messages of self-care.

Depression was the theme for 2001, and then the team chose it again for 2002. The theme for 2003 was spirituality and purpose, while 2004's theme was "Health for Every Body," a nontraditional approach to issues of weight, exercise, health, and food.

Because 90 percent of Mercy's employees are women who have chosen caregiving as a profession in individualistic, independent Iowa, self-care can be a hard sell. Surveyed anonymously, employees admitted to depression, fatigue, and violent relationships, but it's something else entirely to show up for a program on depression, for example, or for counseling. Laura McKibbin reflects on the team's struggle to establish the program:

> Every year we talk about how hard it is. And we get lots and lots of resistance. Blatant, rude resistance, in the beginning, like, "This is a stupid program, and why are we wasting resources on this when we are having a hard time taking care of our patients?" and "It won't last six months." And now it's more "I don't have time to go," which we think is a huge improvement.

Kelly Putnam relates the team's journey with the depression initiative:

> First attempts at targeting depressed employees with screenings, education, and EAP promotions were met with less-than-spectacular results. So instead of addressing depressed employees directly, we trained all Mercy employees in how to be more supportive of *other* people who might be depressed. The switch in approach worked. Interest and participation in the workplace depression initiative exploded.[47]

The free individual counseling offered by Kailo also exploded, often with women seeking counseling who had never sought counseling before. Pre- and posttested, several dozen employees have reduced their symptoms of depression.

The Kailo team keeps alive previous years' themes. They market themselves on individual and organizational health and effectiveness. They package their offerings palatably. For example, the "Kailo-to-Go" menu features "Peace-and-Quiet Appetizers," fifteen- to thirty-minute experiential exercises led by Kailo staff for departmental staff meetings; "Well-Done Entrees" like Optimistic Pizza and Beyond Bootstraps, thirty- to fifty-minute sessions for inservices, staff meetings, or lunch'n'learns; and "Desserts to Dial For," thirty-minute sessions on relationships. Each menu item is served with food. Recently the Kailo team has added an adaptation of the book *First, Break All the Rules: What the World's Greatest Managers Do Differently*[48] as well. Based on Gallup's survey of over eighty thousand managers, the book provides practical suggestions for improving effectiveness in the workplace. The Kailo team has translated the book into "bite-size" workshops, tailored for Mercy Medical employees.

The Kailo team practices what they preach. They focus on self-care and staff development within their own department. For example, when the Kailo theme for the year was sleep, Kailo staff attended to their own sleep, even when they found it challenging to tear themselves away from their work and stop burning the candle at both ends. The team holds an annual planning retreat, hosted by Maxine Brinkman, the team leader, in which they go off-site and spend time in strategic planning, nurturing one another, and eating good food and socializing. Laura McKibbin reports:

> We start with the mission of the hospital, then with Kailo's mission, then focus on our own daily work. One of the things about our department is it's just full of people with passion and energy. Maxine is really good at passion and at growing people and making them feel good about themselves.

Finally, the Kailo team attends a national wellness seminar together annually, held in Stevens Point, Wisconsin, with internationally known resource people.

The Kailo team hold themselves accountable. They track the financial side of the Kailo program, doing cost-benefit analysis, and reporting to Mercy's administration. Kailo staff member Kelly Putnam reported on the financial analysis of the depression initiative in an article in *AWHP's Worksite Health:*

> For the employer, depression has been found by the Health Enhancement Research Organization (HERO) to be the most costly modifiable risk factor with regard to individual, short-term annual health-care claims. HERO data suggests depressed employees cost approximately $1500 more per year than nondepressed employees.
>
> What's more, employees experiencing depression and stress (and many times they go together) cost approximately 70 percent more per year than nondepressed and nonstressed employees.
>
> ...More than forty [Mercy] employees have gone from depressed to nondepressed. The cost-savings, using by-proxy measures from the literature, are estimated at more than $200,000 in reduced short-term health-care claims costs and regained productivity.[49]

Mercy Medical, then, lives in alignment with its mission. An organization clear about its vision and knowing how to get to where it wants to go, Mercy Medical lives its values. From its mission leader serving on the Senior Leadership Team, to its day-to-day recognitions and celebrations, to its outstanding Kailo program, Mercy Medical walks its talk.

Our Lady's Hospice

Our Lady's Hospice, founded in Dublin by the Sisters of Charity in 1879, has served Dublin's sick poor for a century and a quarter. Originally one small building providing palliative care for nine patients, dying poor carried from Dublin's tenements, Our Lady's Hospice has grown to a two-hundred-bed institution providing palliative care, extended care, and rheumatology rehabilitation to fifteen hundred patients a year. In addition, Our Lady's Hospice sponsors an extensive home-care hospice program.

Caring and compassion, the heart of the Sisters' mission to the sick poor, are embedded in the DNA of Our Lady's Hospice. Mary

Aikenhead (1787–1858), responding to the grinding poverty of early-nineteenth-century Dublin, founded the Irish branch of the Religious Sisters of Charity in 1815 in order to serve "God's nobility — the suffering poor."[50] In addition to vows of poverty, chastity, and obedience, the Sisters of Charity took a fourth vow, a vow of service to the poor. These first sisters ministered to the poor of Dublin in their homes, in orphanages, in hospitals, and in prisons. Typhus and cholera epidemics spread like wildfire through Dublin's crowded, unsanitary tenements. The Sisters of Charity nursed the poor during these epidemics, often able to do little more than ease their suffering as they died. Seeing this widespread suffering convinced Mary Aikenhead to found a hospital for the poor, so that "the poor might be given for love what the rich obtain for money."[51] Despite many obstacles, not the least of which was that Dublin's powerful did not approve of either a hospital run by Catholic women or a hospital for the poor in the prestigious Stephen's Green area, St. Vincent's Hospital opened its doors in 1835. The Sisters trained nurses and raised the status of nursing in nineteenth-century Dublin, and gained experience in caring for the sick and dying.

In 1879 — when the Sister of Charity novitiate moved to another location, thus freeing the space that had housed it — the Sisters' long-held dream of opening a hospice became a reality. Sister Mary John Gaynor, aided by a gift of six hundred pounds, converted the novitiate into a hospice and admitted the first patients to Our Lady's Hospice in December of the same year. With space for only 9 patients, the number of applicants soon far exceeded the number of beds available, and Sister Mary John succeeded in raising the funds to build a new facility on the same grounds. The new building opened in 1888, with space for 110 patients.

Mission

Unlike HealthEast and Mercy Medical, which have each experienced many transitions over the past two decades, Our Lady's Hospice was run by the Sisters of Charity for nearly a century and a quarter, until 2002. In 2002, the Irish Sisters of Charity transferred ownership of the institution to lay leadership, to the board of directors of Our Lady's Hospice, LLC.

Whenever employees, patients, families, or students studying palliative care at Our Lady's Hospice are asked, "To what do you attribute the caring, compassionate atmosphere at Our Lady's Hospice?" the most frequent response is "the Sisters." How has the mission of the Sisters been transmitted and kept alive, despite their declining numbers?

First and foremost, they have lived it, and through their example have taught others to live it. For example, the Sisters never pass anyone in the hall without smiling and saying hello. Their love for staff and patients shines through all they do, and thus acts like the trim tab on a boat rudder — small in size, yet big in leverage. In addition, their love and compassion are contagious, serving as leaven throughout the institution. As Michael Connolly, lecturer in nursing, puts it,

> One of the things that still strikes me about this place is that it's a home, as opposed to a hospital. And even if you've been here before, you walk in the doors and there's an incredible presence and peacefulness, which still strikes you.

Despite the large impact from small numbers, the Sisters have recognized the cultural shift, that people are expressing their service to the poor in other ways, not having gone through formation with the Sisters of Charity, and that these are the people who will be carrying forward the mission of Our Lady's Hospice. In a few years, there will no longer be any Sisters of Charity working at Our Lady's Hospice, so the Sisters have had to create other ways of passing on the vision.

The Sisters believe that laypeople can live the love as well as they themselves have in the past, and they have sought to put into writing some of the principles that they always relied on the documents of their community for. Furthermore, they have tried to put into the hiring process some of the discernment they learned through their own discernment about entering the Order. And finally, they have tried to put into the mission training process some of what they received in their formation process in the Order.

The Sisters have articulated the mission thus: "Our Lady's Hospice, founded in 1879 by the Sisters of Charity, strives through a team approach and in an atmosphere of loving care to promote wholeness of body, mind and spirit." The core values of dignity, compassion, justice, quality, and advocacy complement the mission. A mission committee, composed of hospice staff representing all departments and chaired by a board member, seeks to promote awareness of the mission within Our Lady's Hospice and seeks to encourage lay ownership of the mission. The committee also monitors and audits the performance of the hospice from the perspective of values and mission. The committee recently hosted a forum for department heads and ward managers to discuss the role of the mission committee in promoting values and mission, and to discuss the booklet *Keep the Spirit of Our Lady's Hospice Alive,* which had been distributed to all staff. The committee also organizes tours of the Heritage Center on the grounds, seeking to keep staff in touch with the history of the Sisters and of Our Lady's Hospice.

In hiring, Our Lady's Hospice managers seek people who resonate with the mission. Above all, a candidate must exhibit "loving care." Skills can be learned, but values and attitudes must already be part and parcel of who the person is. Make no mistake; it's not that Our Lady's Hospice hires unqualified employees just because they have the right attitude. On the contrary, since Our Lady's Hospice is known as such a good place to work, many qualified applicants apply for each opening. New hires are chosen for congruence with the mission.

All new hires then receive mission training. The Mission Effectiveness training program consists of two parts. In Unit One, Sisters and others introduce new staff to the spiritual and philosophical underpinnings of the institution. Partly the story of the founding and subsequent development of Our Lady's Hospice, partly the story of the Sisters of Charity, the orientation imbues new staff with the rich heritage and spiritual foundations of Our Lady's Hospice and helps staff reflect on how Our Lady's Hospice puts its principles into practice. For example, the cover of the mission booklet features a quotation from Neville Hobson, "Kindness means doing a lot of little things kindly and always; not just a big thing now and then." New staff frequently comment that the mission effectiveness training is their favorite part of new staff orientation. After working at Our Lady's Hospice for a few months, staff are eligible for Unit Two of Mission Effectiveness, which provides a deeper understanding of the values inherent in the Religious Sisters of Charity health services, as well as help in implementing those values.

Ongoing care and supervision also help new hires experience the ethos and live it out themselves. Michael Connolly relates his early experience:

> When you came with your paperwork, nobody was too busy to help you, to make sure that you were going to get paid on time, to make sure that you were settling in okay. You were met at the door and given a tour and shown the places that you needed to go to work, to training, where you'd get breakfast, and then you would go onto the ward and the ward manager was introduced to you and you were given somebody to actually mentor you in your first couple of weeks.

Mentors are carefully chosen to convey the mission in action:

> My ward manager was very dynamic; her vision and enthusiasm and joy were infectious. She also led a project on nursing development and really enthused us all about what nursing was about.

The mission committee also provides ongoing support for keeping the mission alive in the organization. It sponsors social, seasonal, and spiritual celebrations. It encourages open and honest communication to build trusting relationships. It works with management to implement suggestions arising from the Mission Effectiveness programs, and reports, "Many of these suggestions have resulted in improving the physical and working environment of Our Lady's Hospice."[52]

Holistic Patient Care

Holistic patient care characterizes Our Lady's Hospice. Not only do patients receive state-of-the-art medical care to address their physical symptoms, they also receive emotional and spiritual care through the work of a multidisciplinary team. This integrated, shared-care model of palliative care serves the multifaceted needs of the patient and an educational function as well. Dr. Michael Kearney, former medical director at Our Lady's Hospice, argues for the "impact the combined approach of multi-professional expertise and compassionate attention to the whole person can make."[53] He claims:

> We can make the process of dying easier by expertly controlling an individual's pain and other physical symptoms, . . . [while also] working with the deep, inner aspects of a dying person's experience [which is] essentially a cooperative venture with the healing forces of the person's own psyche. This inner depth work is the essential complement to the outer care of the individual.[54]

Dr. Kearney's book, *Mortally Wounded: Stories of Soul Pain, Death, and Healing,* outlines the process of this inner depth work, drawn from his years of working with the dying. He argues that the time of dying is a special time in a person's life, and that if a patient is treated only from a medical perspective, the opportunities for reconciliation and healing that spring from a person's psyche will often be missed. Western culture, he maintains, does not understand "soul pain," and thus needs to learn how to address it so that the whole person can be honored at the end of life.

In 1987, because of its leading role in palliative care, Our Lady's Hospice established an education and research department. In partnership with University College, Dublin, their department now offers three postgraduate higher diplomas in nursing studies: in palliative care, in gerontology, and in rheumatology. In addition, the department offers various other courses and workshops, ranging from the more technical, like the syringe driver workshop, to a course on reminiscence therapy, to a summer school on meditation. The department also runs annual conferences on palliative care, gerentological nursing, and a symposium on rheumatology rehabilitation. In partnership with the human resources department and the mission committee, the department seeks, in its courses and workshops to meet the needs of Our Lady's Hospice employees as well as participants from the outside. Nurses, social workers, physiotherapists, doctors, chaplains, and complementary therapist and care assistants are among those who have benefited from workshops and courses.

Because of its cutting-edge position in palliative care, both in terms of multidisciplinary teams and in terms of whole-person care, Our Lady's Hospice has much to teach those working in health care. Furthermore, whole-person care necessitates whole-person teaching and learning, an approach often not encountered by health-care professionals before participating in courses at Our Lady's Hospice. As Education Coordinator Marianne McGiffin puts it, "If nurses are going to be present to the dying not only physically but also emotionally and spiritually, they need to do their own emotional and spiritual work." To that end, students consider their own biographies in terms of death and dying: What experiences of death and grieving do they have in their own lives? Do they have ungrieved grief? Such explorations take students deep into their own hearts and souls and prepare them to meet patients heart to heart and soul to soul.

Our Lady's Hospice, then, continues to live the charism of Mary Aikenhead and the Sisters of Charity. Through Our Lady's Hospice's caring atmosphere, its holistic patient care, and its spreading the word through the training of students, the Sisters of Charity's charism will continue long after the Sisters are gone.

CONCLUSION

From Ireland to Iowa, then, health-care organizations experiment with how to integrate spirituality throughout the life of their institutions. By focusing on the mission and carefully attending to how to put the mission into effect in their day-to-day life together, these three institutions demonstrate that it is indeed possible to live out their mission, vision, and values, if not perfectly, then at least faithfully and consistently. Furthermore, they demonstrate that the mission can be lived out both externally, in relation to their clients, and internally, in how they treat one another.

Chapter 7

KEEPING GROUNDED

Remembering the Cause behind the Causes

❧❦❧

SISTERS OF THE ROAD CAFÉ

The spirit at Sisters has kept me alive over the years. It's helped keep
me alive spiritually, physically, and mentally. I've never felt alienated
at Sisters of the Road Café.

These words of a customer pay tribute to the community at Sisters of
the Road Café, introduced in part 1 through the leadership of Genny
Nelson. Sisters began its life in 1979 in Portland, Oregon. Its mission
statement reads:

Sisters of the Road Café exists to build authentic relationships and
alleviate the hunger of isolation in an atmosphere of nonviolence and
gentle personalism that nurtures the whole individual toward changes
that will reach the root of his or her homelessness and poverty and
end it forever.

As the mission statement reflects, relationships lie at the heart of
Sisters of the Road. To illustrate why, Genny Nelson refers to a "family mapping" workshop that Sisters of the Road hosted. She first notes
how social service agencies exist to serve particular needs, and that
once those needs are met, clients don't meet the criteria for walking
through the door. However, clients have a different perspective:

You and I might put our mom and our dad and our siblings and all
other extended family on our family map. Many people who are dealing with homelessness have lost all those connections. Who shows
up on their family map? In Portland, Oregon, it's Sisters of the Road
Café, the Glisan Street Shelter, Mental Health Services West, the Public
Health Clinic.

103

Once clients' needs are met, they lose their family. In founding Sisters of the Road, Genny Nelson and Sandy Gooch wanted to create a place in which a customer's search for family would be honored and assisted, not undermined:

> We always stress that Sisters is a little nonprofit restaurant, not a social service agency.... You can walk in the door of Sisters wounded by any number of things. You can be hungry, you can be looking for a place to live, you can be without a job and on and on and on. You can solve those problems and still walk back through the door because we're a little restaurant. You've made friends there. We've got the best twenty-five-cent cup of coffee in town.

At Sisters, many customers have been around for more than a decade, and a few for the entire twenty-five years of its existence. Sisters has seen many customers get back on their feet and start giving back to the community. And they can still come back through the doors of the restaurant for that "best twenty-five-cent cup of coffee in town."

Not surprisingly, Sisters of the Road grew out of relationships. As noted in part 1, Genny Nelson and Sandy Gooch spent over one hundred hours in conversation with homeless people in the Oldtown/ Chinatown neighborhood of Portland in order to discover what they felt they needed. Out of those conversations emerged Sisters of the Road Café, with its three goals of (1) creating a safe and welcoming space, especially for women and children, (2) serving nourishing meals at low cost or in exchange for work, and (3) offering job training and employment. With the philosophy of nonviolence, gentle personalism, and community organizing, Sisters seeks to achieve these goals in its daily life and work.

Building on the description of the philosophy introduced in part 1, nonviolence at Sisters is defined as "a resounding NO to violence of any kind," including such things as physical and verbal assault, class superiority, racism, sexism, and homophobia. Gentle personalism, adopted at Sisters from the Catholic Worker movement, "is profoundly about love":

> We will take personal responsibility for mutual aid to our local, national, and global sisters and brothers wherever human rights are

threatened. We can build compassionate, dignified, and respectful relationships with one another, while steadfastly standing up for each
other's freedom.

Community organizing, according to Genny Nelson, is "never doing
for others what they can do for themselves."

How do this mission and philosophy get lived out in the day-to-day
life of Sisters of the Road? How do the values get put into practice?

First, Sisters serves over three hundred meals a day, building community with every meal. A team of staff, volunteers, and customers
prepares, serves, and cleans up after each day's meal. The hired staff for
the meal program at Sisters of the Road consists of two cooks, a dish-
washer, a cashier, and a floor manager; these positions are often filled
by people who first walked in the door as customers and worked their
way up. Volunteers help for one to two hours in a variety of positions:
assisting the cook, serving food, or helping to wash dishes and clean up
after meals. And finally, since customers themselves can either pay for a
meal or work for a meal, many choose the barter option, either coming
in and working on the spot or using meal credits they have accumulated
through working. Staff, volunteers, and customers work together respectfully. All staff and volunteers receive training in nonviolence and
gentle personalism, and customers are oriented to Sisters' philosophy
and practices the moment they walk through the door. As noted in
part 1, unacceptable behavior is interrupted and viewed as a teachable
moment. At least as important as the meals provided each day from
10:00 to 2:45 is the daily opportunity to live the philosophy and to
build community. Staff, volunteers, and customers alike find that living
out nonviolence and gentle personalism requires constant practice.

Second, the workforce development program helps customers get
back on their feet. Like Greyston Bakery, Sisters of the Road hires
from within whenever possible. But there aren't enough jobs at Sisters for everyone who needs employment. So Sisters has instituted
the workforce development program to support people's efforts to
reenter the workforce. The program helps each participant create an
individualized plan to meet that person's needs. For example, one
person might need help with crafting a resumé while another might

need counseling for anger management. As a former associate director responsible for workforce development says, "So many of our participants never received basic parenting. I'm parenting them — teaching them to shower, shave, and wash their clothes before they go to a job interview." While each participant receives an individualized plan, requirements for participation in the program are uniform for all:

> a commitment to practicing Sisters of the Road's philosophy, the building of strong relationships with co-workers and customers, and the mastery of requisite job skills while operating as part of a team.

Just as the café itself grew out of conversations with people in the neighborhood, so have new programs at Sisters. For example, Crossroads, started in March 2002, identifies itself as a "people's organization committed to identifying and implementing immediate and long-term solutions to problems faced by homeless people both locally and nationwide." Started through conversations among people who had been or were currently homeless, Crossroads represents an effort to bring homeless people's voices into the search for solutions to homelessness. While membership in Crossroads is open to anyone, the majority of leadership comes from those who have experienced homelessness personally.

Crossroads holds weekly action meetings to which all are welcome and in which participants plan actions to combat homelessness. The group plans educational events, political lobbying, and direct actions. For example, the "Right to Sleep" alliance (which includes Crossroads and two other groups) held a direct action in front of Portland's City Hall in March 2004. Following the event, participants spoke to the mayor and city commissioners in the city council chambers. As a result, Crossroads members are now involved with pilot proposals to combat homelessness, in dialogue with city officials. Educational efforts include street theater, FAQs about homelessness on the Crossroads Web site, and a newsletter.

Sisters, in addition to Crossroads, started a research project at the same time, funded in part by the City of Portland. It was introduced this way by city commissioner Eric Sten:

With as much as we have done, we cannot solve the homeless problem simply with social services, as important as these services are. We now need to take the next step and involve the people whose lives are most affected by homelessness and ask them to provide guidance and leadership. That is what Sisters of the Road Café is all about — reflecting the dignity within so that people can flourish and make changes.

Consistent with other programs at Sisters, the research project is committed to doing research *with* people affected by homelessness, rather than *on* them. The six hundredth and final interview was completed in March 2004, and the project is currently focused on data analysis in preparation for three publications: (1) the results of the project, (2) a manual on how to replicate the project, and (3) an anthology of photos and stories culled from the interviews.

At the heart of Sisters of the Road Café, then, lie relationships. Sisters builds relationships with, among others, customers, volunteers, staff, donors, businesses participating in the workforce development program, and the City of Portland. After twenty-five years of working in the community, it's not unusual for the relationships to resurface in unexpected ways. The last time Genny Nelson was seeking a place to live, she called a rental office and the man on the other end responded:

> You're not going to remember me, but I sure know who you are. I came through Sisters looking for a job, and you always called me by name and you guys always asked me about how the job search was going. I'm the manager of this rental office now.

She got the apartment.

SOPHIA HOUSING ASSOCIATION

> Wisdom [*Sophia*] builds a house,
> Understanding establishes a home.
> Knowledge furnishes the rooms
>   with all that is precious and pleasing.
>   — Proverbs 24:3–4

Taking her inspiration from the book of Proverbs, Sr. Jean Quinn, a Daughter of Wisdom, established Sophia Housing in response to a

crying need she witnessed in Dublin. Trained as a nurse and coun-
selor, Jean Quinn had been working with a housing agency for
fourteen years when she felt called to found Sophia Housing. Noting
the lack of holistic programs for the homeless, Quinn observed the
cycle of homelessness repeating itself generation after generation. She
wanted to interrupt the cycle of poverty by providing not only housing but also training in life skills and job skills, all in the context of
spiritual community. Sophia Housing was born in 1997, articulating
its mission thus:

> The mission of Sophia Housing Association is to work alongside
> people outside of home in a holistic way. Our aim is to support
> marginalised, vulnerable and disadvantaged women, men and children
> to become independent through a weaving of programmes that will
> provide support, education and advocacy for them.

Originally a vision of a small community living and praying and
working in Dublin's inner city, the concept of holistic housing spread
like wildfire, and now Sophia Housing exists in twelve locations
across Ireland.

What does this house that Wisdom is building look like? Wisdom's
house started with a foundation of prayer, and soon took an unexpected turn. In addition to Jean's own prayer and the prayer of others
involved, one of Jean's Sisters, a Daughter of Wisdom in England,
took on Sophia Housing as a special prayer ministry. After praying
for years about the germ of the idea of a small community living and
working together, she heard from Jean that all kinds of buildings and
land and money were coming in. "Listen, you have to take it easy,"
Jean told her. "They're coming in fast and furious." Religious orders across Ireland, whose members were declining, had caught the
vision of Sophia Housing and were offering to donate their buildings and land. Jean, committed to working in partnership, accepted
the donations only on the condition that the religious orders would
stay involved in the ministry. The results surprised her. She discovered that religious communities who had been perceiving themselves
as on the brink of extinction suddenly experienced new life being
breathed into them. As Jean talked with them about their ministries of

education or health care that their buildings had formerly supported, they came to see how their charisms could continue to be lived out in ministry to the homeless. Their buildings would continue to house their ministries, but in a different form. Education and health care formed integral parts of Sophia Housing's vision, and the religious orders could contribute their years of expertise. For her part, Jean welcomed partnerships with people who had been serving their local communities for generations, who knew the needs and were part of local networks.

In addition to partnership, the other trademark of Sophia Housing is a Wisdom Centre in every building. Though expensive to build, Jean sees the Wisdom Centre as representing the heart of Sophia's holistic model:

> My biggest dream was to build a Wisdom Centre. I knew that as part of the holistic way of working with homeless people, we needed to have a place where people could come comfortably for counseling, for some of the alternative therapies they could never afford, for a meeting space, for a reflective space, a place of serenity within the community.

Early in the planning stage of the first building, Jean asked the architect how much it would cost to build the Wisdom Centre she envisioned. When he responded, "About half a million," she had no idea where she would get the money. Three weeks later, to the day, she received a call offering an unsolicited donation of more than enough to cover the cost.

Jean Quinn and Eamonn Martin now serve as co-CEOs of Sophia Housing, modeling the shared leadership that lies at the heart of Sophia's model. The philosophy of partnership gets lived out throughout the organization. The board consists of twelve people, six of whom are religious from sponsoring congregations, six of whom are lay, bringing a variety of gifts. Sophia's sixty staff members, most of whom are part-time, work in teams facilitated by project leaders. Teams meet weekly, not only to focus on tasks, but also to look at themselves as a team and strengthen their relationships. Everyone in the organization receives supervision, Jean and Eamonn from outside the organization, then Jean supervises the two managers and some project leaders. One of the managers supervises the other project leaders, and project leaders in turn supervise those in their teams.

Gatherings and celebrations occur regularly at Sophia Housing. Once a year, everyone across the organization gathers for an agency day. An outside facilitator leads the group through reflection on how it is living out its mission and helps teams establish goals for the year ahead. The day also serves as a time for employees to get to know one another better, to discover what has been going on in one another's lives. The day ends with a celebration of all that has been accomplished in the past year and an honoring of employees. Every June, the entire organization gathers again for a birthday celebration for Sophia. Themes differ from year to year, from a fun day one year, to reflection in the Wisdom Centre another year, to making pottery another year. In addition, Sophia holds celebrations for individual employees' birthdays and anniversaries as well as holiday celebrations for such days as Christmas, Easter, St. Patrick's Day, and Valentine's Day.

We've seen what Wisdom's house looks like internally. What does it look like on the outside, in what it offers its clients? In envisioning Sophia Housing, Jean began by asking the simple question, "What do people need?" Her answer: they need an adequate physical environment, they need emotional support, they need practical help, and they need spiritual nurture. Sophia Housing provides all of these. From the first contact with Sophia, through the application process and interview, through the pre-tenancy preparation, through the moving into housing and beyond, clients experience Sophia's holistic approach. Clients learn from the beginning that Sophia staff want to get to know them as people, want to journey with them. After the application process and interview, clients enter pre-tenancy preparation, a three- to six-week period of getting to know Sophia Housing as Sophia Housing gets to know them. They meet with a staff person twice a week to address issues that may get in the way of their successfully navigating the transition from being homeless to being housed. They enter the groups that will accompany them into their transitional housing. The groups, facilitated by a staff person, focus on a number of areas. First, they address practicalities such as budgeting, cooking, housekeeping, and basic parenting skills. Second, they help clients understand and make informed choices about their sexuality, address violence against women, and educate about addictions. Third, as the groups continue to journey together, Sophia staff invite local politicians to visit, teaching clients how the social and political system works. Such learning helps clients become empowered to enter into the system and make it work for them instead of being disenfranchised. It also introduces politicians to the population served by Sophia Housing, allowing them to see people who would otherwise be invisible to them. Fourth, the groups introduce participants to the arts, taking them to art museums, the theater, and concerts. Sophia Housing views the arts as one means of healing. Jean Quinn illustrates with the story of a woman who never spoke up in her group when participants were sharing their life stories. One day they went to the art museum. After talking over coffee about what they could expect to see, they all went off and looked at the pictures. When they regathered over coffee and shared what it was like for them to look at the art, Jean relates,

> Well, this woman started, "I saw a picture and it helped me remember," and then she started to tell us her story and she never stopped after that.

Finally, the groups take participants out in nature. Many clients have never been outside of Dublin, and going to the mountains or forest can be intimidating at first, but usually eventually results in an expanding of horizons and occasionally contributes to a healing of the soul.

For Jean and the other staff and contributing organizations, Sophia Housing does not just address needs in the world, it addresses their own needs as well. This is one of the characteristics of soul at work, where the purpose of the organization embraces all its members and stakeholders. The soul of the organization thus sustains and feeds the souls of those who constitute it, grounding the work of the organization in the work to which its individuals are called.

Shalem Institute for Spiritual Formation

In 1973 a small group of people yearning for a deeper, more contemplative way of relating to God began meeting weekly in Washington, D.C. Facilitated by Tilden Edwards, an Episcopal priest, the group consisted of clergy and laypeople from various Christian traditions, open to interfaith dialogue with other deep spiritual traditions. As the group grew, new groups formed, and this growing network of groups sponsored retreats and workshops. The Shalem Institute for Spiritual Formation, made up of these groups, incorporated in 1979 under the leadership of Edwards and began sponsoring, in addition to retreats and workshops, an enrichment program for spiritual directors. Now a thriving organization with nine office staff, nearly forty program staff, four long-term programs, and various short-term offerings, Shalem articulates its mission thus:

> The mission of the Shalem Institute is to be an ecumenical community responding to a call to help mediate God's Spirit in the world through the loving wisdom of contemplative tradition.

From the beginning, Shalem has sought to integrate its contemplative approach to spirituality not only into its program offerings but also into its life as an organization.

The structures and processes put into place during Shalem's early years have changed and grown as Shalem as grown. Shalem, as an organization, has always attempted to allow the Spirit to guide organizational life. Aware that institutions can become self-perpetuating even when the life has gone out of them, Shalem leaders have sought to ensure that the institutional structures continue to serve the mission, rather than the other way around. Although they have often found this goal difficult to attain, they continue to struggle toward it. Tilden Edwards, Shalem's former executive director, reflected, upon his retirement after twenty-seven years in the position:

> [The role of executive director] has taught me empathy for executives in other organizations, as I have traversed the spiritual and managerial pitfalls, mistakes, and never-ending decisions about programs, policies, staffing, and crises over the years. I have tried, not always successfully,

to trust the Spirit's aliveness in our evolving organizational life: in its dilemmas and actions, joys and pains, surprises and predictabilities. The job has been a fierce teacher of humility, listening discerningly, learning when to act and when to wait, and the necessity of self-examination and courage related to the kinds of personal presence called for amidst many organizational interactions.[55]

Shalem staff seek to bring a prayerful, attentive presence to staff meetings. As they have experimented with various ways of doing this, they have discovered, among other things, that if a meeting goes for more than twenty minutes without a break for silence, it is likely that ego has taken over.

In reflecting on Shalem's commitment to a prayerful presence in meetings, current co-executive director Carole Crumley relates how the practice of passing a stone around the group and asking the one who holds it to be in silent prayer, affected her:

Inevitably I would have a stake in some item on the agenda and usually I would get the prayer stone at the moment we came to that item. I discovered that just being in prayer for that item was an enormous contribution. Maybe that was my best contribution.

Bill Dietrich, the other current co-executive director, also experiences the power of prayerful attentiveness in meetings. At the same time, he acknowledges the difficulty of consistently practicing it. For example:

When people start talking about money it's amazing how prayerfulness can just go right out the window. I can recall times when we just went headlong into our conversation for an hour and got finished with the meeting and said, "Oops."

Over the years, Shalem has changed its structures and processes to accommodate new needs. For example, in 1995 staff undertook an extensive examination and discernment about their internal structure. Discerning that a team structure better fit their philosophy and relationships than did the traditional hierarchical structure they had inherited, staff made the transition to teams. The restructuring resulted in a program team overseeing Shalem's programs, a business team overseeing the business side of Shalem, and an executive team stewarding Shalem's overall health and future vision.[56] Not only did roles and responsibilities change to reflect more accurately team members' gifts and contributions, financial compensation also changed. Patricia Clark, director of development at the time, relates her struggle with accepting a lower salary:

> I found myself eyeball to eyeball with my colleagues on the Business Team, knowing my higher salary was a key point. . . . The night before a crucial salary meeting and what it meant as a team, I went home, prayed and got real clarity about my security, that all was possible in a world full of God's abundant love, and that I need worry about nothing. This was not an ethereal feeling; it was very practical and solid. I knew what I could give up financially. The team came together the next day and worked out a formula using the salary money of the team to be divided in a new way recognizing equality of responsibility, the value of each person's gifts, experience and longevity. The formula matched my practical prayer answer exactly.[57]

Staff felt that the transition to teams was very successful, despite the bumps along the way. Productivity and morale increased, as did the sense of teamwork and shared ownership. Diane Paras, fundraiser at the time, attributed the ability to change to the staff's spirituality:

> We believe we recognized the need for this change and were able to accommodate it because of the contemplative dimension of our time together. As a praying community, listening in unison to God's call, spirituality in the workplace became more than a topic of conversation, more than a shared desire. It was our struggle to function in the workplace contemplatively that brought us to the team structure. Only by taking an open, flexible, and trusting stance could power and responsibility be shared to such a great extent.[58]

The later significant growth of Shalem staff and programs led to the need for a different, more ordered staff decision-making structure, but the essential value of a prayerful process of discernment in meetings, including frequent times of silence, has never been lost.

In 2000, when founder Tilden Edwards retired after twenty-seven years of service, the transition to the new executive director had been prepared for by more than a year of prayer and discernment. Visitors to Shalem's Web site were invited to pray for the process of selecting a new executive director, and the search committee did its work with an attitude of prayerful discernment. Applicants for the position were asked to write about their sense of call and the place of prayerfulness in leadership, as well as about specific skills they had for the job. The interview process for finalists included prayer with the search committee and questions about how the candidate would nurture spirituality in Shalem's organizational life.

When the new executive director stayed less than two years, the temptation for Shalem staff and board was to ask, "Why did God let us down?" or "What did we do wrong?" Instead, because of their years of deep attentiveness and prayer together, despite the bumps and challenges, Shalem folks were able to remember that the discernment process is not a template that guarantees certain results. They were able to turn to God again and ask, "What is God doing here?" While the process of filling the interim position and eventually the permanent position wasn't always easy, staff and board members were reminded that God continued to walk with them.

At Shalem, we see how the faithful and consistent spiritual grounding of the organization consistently opens possibilities for creative solutions and resolutions that would otherwise be invisible. One of the fruits of spiritual grounding is the patience to listen for unexpected solutions, leading to answers which are out of the box.

CONCLUSION

Nonprofits nearly always begin as labors of love, addressing needs in the world that their founders are called to address. On the surface, these needs might seem to be the soul of the organization, its driving impetus. While this is partially true, the life of the organization proceeds from its members' callings and needs as well, and these are served by the organization as surely as the bottom line of the needs it addresses. In the examples of this chapter, we have seen how organizations are as much about the community they create as they are about the communities they serve. This chemistry allows them to thrive, adapt, and survive the inevitable changes thrust upon them.

Chapter 8

HOW ORGANIZATIONS LISTEN
Corporate Discernment

❧❀❧

Chapter 4 considered individual spiritual discernment as it focused on the leaders introduced in part 1 and on how their discernment practices affected their leadership. This chapter extends to the corporate level chapter 4's explanation of discernment.

What does corporate spiritual discernment look like? The tone of corporate discernment is one of openness and trust: toward one another, toward the transcendent. In order for a group to use corporate discernment in its decision making, it needs to establish a foundation of mutual respect and trust. If a group lacks this, it won't be able to discern together. Once the trust is present, to set the tone of openness to one another and to the transcendent in a meeting, a facilitator will often open with prayer or a meditation. Group members may be asked to share something of their own spirituality with one another, in order to help them become familiar with the spiritual landscape of the group, the ground for their discernment together. They will practice listening deeply to themselves and to one another, learning to discern when to speak and when to remain silent. The focus is on seeking God's wisdom, God's guidance for the situation at hand.[59] They will learn how to listen for this, seeking the deeper wisdom within themselves, hearing it from deep within one another, hearing it in the silent moments in between. They will learn pacing, the appropriate rhythm for discernment, a less hurried pace than that typical of most meetings in business settings. As discernment gradually becomes part of an organization's culture, these practices will become second nature.

At the end of a meeting, a facilitator may invite a group to reflect on its process: Was there a sense of freedom in the group? Was everyone included? Was the whole person included — body, mind, emotions, spirit? Was enough time given for the decision? Was there a sense of unhurried presence?

Corporate discernment is most often discussed and practiced in religious settings. How can it be translated into a diverse business or other organizational setting? How can a practice that is rooted in religion be translated and used with people who represent diverse religious traditions or perhaps no religious tradition?

To answer these questions, let's turn to three of the organizations we met earlier, one a secular manufacturing company, one a religiously affiliated medical center, and one a spiritually based umbrella organization for two businesses and several social service agencies, exploring their cultures and decision-making processes in more depth.

REELL PRECISION MANUFACTURING

In part 1, we met Bob Carlson, co-CEO of Reell Precision Manufacturing. We observed him exercising spiritual discernment in his leadership role. In this chapter, we examine Reell's larger culture, considering how it supports both individual and corporate discernment. We also examine corporate discernment in action at Reell.

Reell Precision Manufacturing, as noted in part 1, is a global designer and manufacturer of intermittent rotary motion products and slip clutch devices. Incorporated in 1970 with very little capital and three employees, it grew to over two hundred employees by the turn of the century. Reell's three cofounders, Dale Merrick, Lee Johnson, and Bob Wahlstedt, started the business with the vision of having a company that would allow them to develop professionally and put family ahead of work. As they grew in their Christian faith, they began to incorporate spiritual principles into the company. By 1972 they had made explicit their commitment to "follow the will of God" in business decisions, to be discerned by prayer and unanimous agreement among the three of them.

How did this commitment to corporate spiritual discernment become manifested in the business arena? It started in the weekly Monday morning breakfast meetings of the three cofounders and then spread to the company as a whole. The three partners found that their commitment to corporate discernment "provided the basis for a working relationship between three unrelated business partners that has been almost totally free of the discord that is typical of such relationships. Since each of us, in effect, [had] veto power, the perspectives of all [had to] be considered and accommodated before a new direction [could] be implemented."[60] This approach, of course, required that each partner be willing to let go of ego and seek what was best for the whole. The partners found that

> We usually [were] able to reach unanimous agreement but sometimes only after several discussions over several days. We found that a day or more [was] often required to fully "digest" the other perspectives and be able to come to a common agreement.[61]

When they were unable to reach agreement, they discovered an important pattern:

> A most interesting effect [arose] when we were unable to agree even after going through this process. We usually [found] that the question [was] wrong! We tried to redefine the question and then [were] able to agree on a direction.... We [now] feel that we have found a practical way of knowing when the wrong question is being asked.[62]

The first major test of this commitment to corporate discernment came in January 1975 when "the roof fell in."[63] During an economic downturn, Reell's sole customer informed them that they already had enough of Reell's product to last them through the year, and they wouldn't be placing any orders for the rest of that year. The spiritual foundation of Reell, which had been resulting in enhanced organizational performance, was no longer doing so. What were they to do? One option suggested was to abandon the spiritual foundation and simply imitate many other companies' response to the economic downturn, such as laying off employees. Perhaps the experiment with building the company on spiritual principles had run its course. Spiritual principles and practices were fine during times of economic boom, but were an unnecessary luxury during a recession. But another option was articulated, and Reell chose that path: perhaps spiritual principles and practices could help Reell *better* weather the economic storm than could conventional business practices. It seemed worth a try.

The three partners brought to their discernment process the question of what to do about layoffs. Even though another contract from a new customer came through in early 1975, it was clear that the 1975 income would not support the 1974 payroll. Though usual business practice would suggest laying people off, through prayer and discussion the partners "sought God's will" until they reached unanimous agreement. The result was surprising. Instead of laying anyone off, the cofounders agreed to ask all employees to take a 10 percent cut in salary or hours worked, while they themselves took a much larger cut. Everyone agreed to the cuts. Before the end of the year, this reduction had to be increased to 20 percent. Morale remained high despite the pay cuts, as employees understood the owners were sacrificing even more than they were. The seed of Reell's philosophy that made the security and growth of employees the highest priority of the company had been planted.

The three partners continued to use their discernment process over the years, finding that it kept them spiritually grounded and focused on what was most important. As a result, it helped them make better business decisions. Corporate discernment was practiced not only among the three partners who met on Monday morning, but also in other settings in the company.

Then, in 1992, Reell faced a significant challenge to its discernment process. For some co-workers (as Reell was calling employees by this time) the very foundation upon which Reell rested seemed to contradict Reell's stated values. The phrase, "Reell is committed to following the will of God," in Reell's Direction Statement left some co-workers feeling excluded. While they felt valued and respected in their day-to-day life at Reell, and while they experienced the lived reality of the part of the Direction Statement that read "to treat the concerns of others (co-workers, customers, and suppliers) equally with our own concerns," they felt that Reell's articulation of an explicit Christian foundation excluded them. Steve Wikstrom, then vice president of manufacturing, heard these concerns and initiated a process by which discernment about (1) what Reell's foundation was and (2) how to best express that foundation could occur.

Initially it seemed that Reell had hit a wall. The old way of discerning when there was an intractable problem, i.e., turning to an explicit corporate commitment to God and seeking God's will, was the very issue at stake. The very spiritual practice that had pulled the company through other hard times and had led to the company's earlier transformations was itself in question. The cofounders had experienced "following the will of God" to be the way to let go of their own egos and find the way forward that was best for the company as a whole. To let go of that phrase seemed to some to be letting go of Reell's entire spiritual foundation. Others, for whom the phrase "following the will of God" had no meaning, felt that there must be another way to express the spiritual foundation that could include them. How were they to find a way forward?

Because of the years of practicing discernment, Reell co-workers knew the experience, even if they described it in different ways. They knew how to be open to one another and listen deeply. They knew how to be open to something beyond themselves. They knew that the process involved a willingness to let go of their own agendas. They knew how to distinguish between stubbornness and a matter of conscience. All this served them well in the process.

Although the process was bumpy, with many ups and downs along the way, the group working on Reell's Direction Statement found a more inclusive way to express the spiritual foundation. More important, it seemed to *better* express what Reell was already doing. It acknowledged the Judeo-Christian values in which the company was rooted, eliminated the phrase "to follow the will of God," and added a phrase "we are challenged to work and make decisions consistent with God's purpose for creation according to our individual understanding." By replacing "follow the will of God" with "we are challenged to work and make decisions consistent with God's purpose for creation according to our individual understanding," the group sought to acknowledge the diversity of spiritualities present at Reell and the richness contributed by various spiritual traditions. Reell had always welcomed spiritual diversity in its hiring and promotion practices; now the Direction Statement reflected this reality.

Reell lived with the revised Direction Statement for over a decade and found it to generate high ownership and satisfaction in the company. In 2004, when the Direction Statement was revised again, the phrase "we are challenged to work and make decisions consistent with God's purpose for creation according to our individual understanding" remained the same.

With the retirement of the three cofounders and the transition to new leadership, the commitment to corporate discernment continued, as did the Monday morning breakfast meetings. Bob Carlson, who became co-CEO in 1998, describes the meetings thus:

> The purpose of the meeting is to seek inspirational wisdom. Now, inspirational wisdom isn't something that you hit a button and it's there, but [the meeting] is a time where we're more reflective and quieter and trying to make space for inspirational wisdom. We try to listen to ourselves and listen to each other, maybe a little harder than we do when things are really busy.

The meetings always end with seven minutes of silence when the three men set the timer and, in Carlson's words, "quit talking and try to listen and hear whatever's there to be heard."

Steve Wikstrom, the other current co-CEO, discovered that this process not only resulted in better business decisions but also has transformed him:

> I came into this company with a strong desire to be the top decision maker, alone in a position of ultimate leadership. Today I don't feel that way at all. I feel the best way to run this organization is with a shared team of top leaders. It teaches you a lot about consensus, humility, and give-and-take.[64]

Corporate discernment continues to be practiced not only among the three who meet weekly, but also in other settings in the company. For example, as noted in part 1, when the company faced the economic downturn of early 2001, the entire cabinet (consisting of eleven people at that time) used the process. Bob Carlson, still a relative newcomer as co-CEO at the time, experienced that difficult time as an opportunity to practice ways of working he had always wanted to try but had never had the opportunity to try in his other work settings. The experience was part of his own formation in the company's culture:

> Certainly going through the business slowdown and being free to navigate the slowdown and use the resources of Reell and use the wisdom of the Reell community was a growing experience for me — going through the whole cycle and getting solid confirmation of what I intuitively felt but didn't get a chance to apply in other environments. ... The way we went through this together and the dialogue we had around how to deal with the 30 percent drop in revenues was a very collaborative process. The wisdom didn't come from any one place. Seeing the power of all that collectivity and seeing the good results was very confirming.

In general, Reell has discovered that individual and corporate discernment work together and nurture one another. The individuals who have learned to "seek inspirational wisdom" bring their deep searching and varied insights to the group, enriching the group's understanding. The group's deep listening and discovery of insights in turn shape the individual participants, who then go out better trained to "seek inspirational wisdom" both on their own and when they face the next group challenge.

MERCY MEDICAL

Mercy Medical Center–North Iowa, introduced in chapter 6, also practices corporate discernment. Practiced by Sisters of Mercy, corporate discernment found its way into Mercy Medical Center through the various Sisters who served in the role of CEO from its founding until 1995. Even after 1995, when the declining number of Sisters with health-care administration experience required the baton to be passed to lay leadership, corporate discernment remained a central practice.

Today the senior leadership team retains the flavor of corporate discernment in all its meetings and more fully practices corporate discernment in selected meetings. Furthermore, other groups within the system also use the practice.

Senior leadership team meetings (consisting of the CEO, the seven vice presidents, the mission leader, and a Sister of Mercy administrative assistant) always open with prayer or a "reflection," setting a tone of openness to the transcendent. Members of the team enter the meeting assuming that they are responsible to something beyond themselves. The presence of the mission leader at senior leadership team meetings is testimony to the commitment to raise questions of the greater purpose in every decision that is made. At Mercy Medical, the mission leader is not just a figurehead but is expected to be a prominent voice in all decision making. As Doug Morse, senior vice president of network and clinic management, puts it:

> Our mission leader sits on the senior leadership team, and is very vocal. So even when we're talking about nursing and personnel issues or anything financial, we have our mission person bringing us back to the larger context, giving us the ever-present reminders and input of the mission side.

A spirit of stewardship pervades senior leadership team meetings, a spirit of holding the institution in trust for its larger purpose.

Whenever a major decision needs to be made, the senior leadership team uses (or delegates a subcommittee to use) a formal corporate discernment practice known as the "mission discernment" process. This formal mission discernment process is a way of "hardwiring" attention to discernment and mission into senior decision-making scenarios. A booklet distributed to the board, the senior leadership team, and various other leaders throughout the system describes the process thoroughly and matter-of-factly.[65] At Mercy Medical, attention to the transcendent is just as important as attention to spreadsheets and clinical issues. Each has its role to play, and they work together in a mutually respectful dialogue.

The booklet details concrete guidelines for using the process, thus providing one way of putting spirituality into practice in the institution. Laid out alongside each phrase of the mission statement, the guidelines ensure that each aspect of the mission will be thoroughly taken into account. For example, under "in the spirit of the Gospel" (the second phrase of the mission statement), the discerning group is instructed to consider prayerfully "How does the initiative under consideration present Trinity Health with opportunities to demonstrate and foster its Mission and Core Values?" Under "to heal body, mind, and spirit" (the third phrase of the mission statement), the group is asked, "How does the proposal under consideration affect the ability of the Trinity Health Member Organization to provide spiritual care?"

In addition to giving the discerning group concrete questions to address, the booklet sets the context by instructing the group about such matters as the purpose and timing of the process:

Purpose

Mission Discernment is a reflective process intended to stimulate discussion among decision-makers that will enable them to identify and report, in mission and values terms, explicit reasons for or against a particular proposed course of action.... The Mission Discernment Process is intended to ensure that, in the course of making major decisions, appropriate business and clinical analyses are evaluated in light of the Mission and Core Values.[66]

Process timing

The process of Mission Discernment begins when a previously discussed possibility or alternative is in need of clear analysis and decision. The process should proceed in conjunction with other components of the project.... The purpose and value of Mission Discernment is missed if the process is employed after all other elements of the deliberation have been concluded.[67]

Recently the mission discernment process was used to consider whether Mercy Medical should open a preadolescent psychiatric services program. Because other Iowa hospitals had closed their programs, children from as far as four hours away were being brought to Mercy's emergency room and then had nowhere to go. CEO

Jim Fitzpatrick assembled a team to use the mission discernment process. Convinced that the process was "expensive (in terms of senior leadership's time) but worth it in the long run (in terms of depth of consideration, spiritual grounding, and buy-in from all sectors)," Fitzpatrick directed Mission Services to facilitate a mission discernment process. The mission leader and mission fellow led a collaborative process, which included the vice president of finance and several behavioral services and emergency room clinicians.

According to senior vice president Doug Morse, a decision that for some groups would have been very easy because "there's no money in it, it requires staff you can't hire and space you don't have" for Mercy required serious wrestling. While the financial and clinical aspects were carefully considered, the discernment team also weighed Mercy's core value of caring for the "poor and underserved," especially women and children. They identified three options: building and opening a preadolescent behavioral program of their own, continuing limited twenty-four- to forty-eight-hour admission for crisis support/stabilization and then transferring patients to facilities in Des Moines, and partnering with a local center to help that program strengthen its services. The team presented their report to the operations team (a subcommittee of the senior leadership team). Based on the thorough values analysis of the mission discernment process, the operations team decided to continue with limited stabilization support with an openness to future collaborative services with the local center, feeling that this option honored Mercy's mission and best served the needs of the children.

The mission discernment process has also been used in several other cases: in relation to a joint venture for an ambulatory surgery center, to consider the question of access to pharmaceutical care in a rural community, and to consider requesting Medicare wage index reclassification. The mission discernment process was started in relation to following the common practice of not accepting patients who have no insurance into a skilled unit. Mission leader Jim Spencer reports,

Moments into the process we determined that this common policy (around the country) was not consistent with our mission. There was no need to continue with a mission discernment.

An illustration of how the mission discernment process is no "magic bullet," these cases also illustrate that

> the consistent use of the Mission Discernment process assures the synthesis and integration of the mission, values, business and clinical impacts of proposed initiatives, thereby promoting responsible decisions. The process cannot offer perfect solutions to complex situations, but...it will enable Trinity Health to make consistent steps in more faithfully fulfilling its mission.... [It] also will help leaders and staff become more adept at identifying mission and values issues in the life and work of the organization.[68]

GREYSTON FOUNDATION

David Rome, senior vice president of the Greyston Foundation, an organization based on Buddhist principles, is the first to admit that integrating the spiritual dimension into a complex organization is not easy. Nevertheless, Greyston has faithfully experimented, for over twenty years, with various ways of doing just that.

Greyston Foundation, introduced in chapter 1, has grown from the original bakery founded in 1982 by Bernie Glassman to the $14 million, 180-employee organization, serving more than two thousand people annually, that it is today. The Greyston Foundation has a well-articulated philosophy that underpins its corporate decision making and discernment. Bernie Glassman, in founding Greyston, adopted the image of a mandala to describe Greyston's mission:

> In Buddhism, the mandala is a circular diagram representing the different aspects of life within a balanced and harmonious whole; it represents the unity and interdependence of life. Within Greyston, the term is used on three levels to denote
>
> - the well-balanced individual
> - the well-functioning community
> - the integration of the individual within community.[69]

Each Greyston organization, each team within an organization, as well as Greyston as a whole, carries in its consciousness the awareness of its interdependence. Pathmaking services, the soul-tending part of Greyston, has developed a "balance" sheet that individuals, departments, and organizations within Greyston use to assess how well they are living out the balance and interdependence represented by the mandala. Such awareness of interdependence provides the foundation for corporate discernment, as it implies that no one person has all the truth but that each has a part of the truth and each must listen for the pieces that others bring.

Furthermore, Greyston stresses community building as an outward manifestation of this interdependence, both within and outside the organization. As Julius Walls puts it:

> We believe the way to overcome social and economic problems, fundamentally, is by building strong community. So Greyston itself has to be a strong community. This is different from the way people think of a traditional nonprofit, where a group of professionals provide services to a group of unfortunates. We are all involved together in creating healthy community.[70]

David Rome underscores the importance of community, noting the tremendous growth "among the so-called professionals, many of whose lives have been turned around from working here," and adding:

> Our mission talks about healing the rejected parts of society as well as the rejected parts of ourselves, so we try not to play into the class system of "us helping them."[71]

With this understanding of interdependence and this experience of community, the stage is set for integrating spiritual practices into decision-making processes. David Rome muses, "For me, it is all about being able to shift gears, slow down, step back, and be contemplative."[72]

Over the years, Greyston has experimented with various practices that help a group "shift gears and be contemplative" in its decision making.

As noted in chapter 4, Bernie Glassman articulated a threefold sequence for perceiving reality: (1) not-knowing, or shedding pre-conceived notions; (2) bearing witness, or gazing steadily at what is; and (3) healing, or taking action that will lead to spiritual transfor-mation. Just as members of the Greyston community have learned to use this discernment process individually, so they have experimented with using it corporately.

The practice of the Way Council is used regularly, not only in Grey-ston Family Support Services (as seen in part 1) and in Greyston Bakery (as seen in chapter 5), but also by various other Greyston groups: in senior management meetings, in large community meet-ings, and in small business-focused discussions. The practice of sitting in a circle, passing around a talking piece, and observing the five guidelines (listening from the heart, speaking from the heart, spon-taneity, being of lean expression, and confidentiality) has served many Greyston groups well. When Greyston's senior management team uses the process, they meet in a special room, different from the one used for regular business meetings. They have found that the practice of the Way of Council trains them in listening deeply and respectfully to one another, and trains them in listening for the transpersonal dimension. Such training sets the tone for letting go of preconceived notions, for bearing witness to what is, and for discerning right action when they come together to do business.

Business meetings themselves begin with silence in order to create space for deep listening. "One of the nice things about silence, which is very much a part of the Buddhist tradition," remarks David Rome, "is that it seems to work for everyone, because there are no words." He notes that while Buddhists meditate during the silence, Christians might pray, and those unaffiliated with a spiritual tradition might take a few moments of reflection. After the silence is a transition period of going around the circle and allowing time for members to check in about how they are feeling that day. Greyston leaders are also cur-rently experimenting with the practice of dialogue as a way to bring more fully into business meetings the three aspects of discernment. Business meetings occasionally close with silence as well.

The Greyston senior management team also takes a quarterly daylong retreat off-site to step back and look at the big picture and, in David Rome's words, "help people become more present in themselves and more present to the group."[73]

When asked to reflect on his most important learning from his work at Greyston, especially with regard to integrating spirituality into organizational processes, David Rome responds, "Hang in there; things take longer than one would expect or like."

CONCLUSION

Reell Precision Manufacturing, Mercy Medical, and the Greyston Foundation all practice various forms of corporate discernment. As noted in chapter 4, studies of American companies show that more than half of all managerial decisions fail, primarily due to leaders giving in to pressures to make decisions too quickly.[74] By incorporating corporate discernment into their decision-making toolkits, these organizations have tried to slow themselves down, take into account more than just financial considerations, and, as a result, make better decisions. Furthermore, with this approach there is no division between winners and losers after the decision is made. These organizations have discovered that corporate discernment is much more likely to result in buy-in from all participants because everyone had a part in the decision. The decisions are better supported and more wholeheartedly implemented than decisions made by edict or coercion.

PART THREE

Putting It All Together

Chapter 9

PUTTING IT ALL TOGETHER
Spiritual Leadership in Organizations

꒰ ꒱

INTRODUCTION

In chapter 1, we saw snapshots of organizations manifesting soul at work. We then went behind the scenes and saw what soulful leadership looks like. We have glimpsed the inner lives of those leaders. We have considered the place of spiritual discernment. And we have considered the organization as a whole, what an organization undergoing spiritual transformation looks like in three different settings: business, health care, and nonprofits.

It's time to address a few difficult questions. Why should an organization want to integrate spirituality into its leadership and organizational life? In order to improve its organizational effectiveness and ultimately its bottom line? This is one good reason. At the same time, if spirituality is ultimately about nonmaterialistic concerns, is it appropriate to focus on the material gains to be reaped by integrating spirituality into organizational life? If an organization adopts spiritual practices in order to improve its bottom line, has it trivialized spirituality? Or has the organization been manipulated or deceived? What happens when the organization that chooses to follow a spiritual path hits the inevitable bumps on the spiritual journey? Will it abandon the spiritual path because it has only a superficial understanding of what spirituality is all about? Will it become cynical about spirituality? Is more harm than good done when an organization adopts spirituality in order to enhance its material gain?

This chapter addresses these questions by considering the process of individual spiritual transformation and by comparing that to organizational transformation through returning to the example of Reell Precision Manufacturing. In particular, the focus is on the motivation for entering upon a spiritual path and what happens when an individual or organization hits the inevitable bumps. What helps an individual or organization make the transition to the second half of the journey, the part of the journey in which the individual or organization understands that the spiritual journey is more about its own transformation than about what material gain it can reap from being on a spiritual path? How can an organization understand this transition it will face and learn to persevere through the second half of the journey?

This chapter begins by offering a condensed version of what spiritual transformation looks like in an individual, drawing out themes that recur again and again in great spiritual teachers. Although details differ across times and places, cultures and traditions, the themes highlighted here occur in the teachings of many diverse spiritual masters. This account uses theistic language, but, as in chapters 4 and 8, it is important to note that a similar account of spiritual transformation could be offered in nontheistic language.[75]

Individual Spiritual Transformation

Most people seem to start out on a spiritual path because of some dissatisfaction with life without spirituality. At first they meet with abundant gifts. Like little children discovering that their parents want them to have good things, these sojourners discover that the spiritual path is a path of generous abundance. Their prayers are answered; they experience God's love and closeness; they feel an exhilaration like that of falling in love.

There is nothing wrong with coming to spirituality because following a spiritual path will make one's life better. There is nothing wrong with coming to spirituality because spirituality will give one what one needs to address one's problems. Members of Alcoholics Anonymous, for example, find that relying on a higher power provides the first step necessary for their recovery. In fact, most seekers come to a spiritual path because of need, believing that through spirituality the need will be met. And they are right.

At the same time, as sojourners continue on the path, they find the ground shifting under their feet. They encounter the transition to the second half of the journey, the part of the spiritual journey in which they transition from thinking that the spiritual journey is about getting gifts to realizing it is about their own transformation. What happens when they find their prayers aren't being answered every time they turn around? What happens when it becomes difficult to pray, when they find the joy and closeness to God they felt in prayer drying up? Often they feel they must be doing something wrong, and they try harder, only to discover even more dryness and frustration. Or they give up on prayer altogether, deciding either that they're not cut out for the spiritual path or that this whole spiritual thing must have been a figment of their imaginations.

However, turning to spiritual teachers reveals that this is a normal and predictable part of the spiritual journey. Spiritual teachers through the ages have observed that in the early days of a seeker's spiritual journey God (in theistic language) is so delighted that he is praying at all that God showers him with answers to his prayers. As time goes on, God cares enough about the seeker to invite him to a deeper place. His first form of prayer dries up so that he can discover a new form. This is when he moves to the second half of the journey. He learns that the spiritual journey is more about his transformation than it is about getting the things he wants from a gift-giver God. He learns to listen to God and let God shape his prayers. Maturing spiritually involves embracing and letting go, embracing and letting go, time and again: of ways of prayer, of relationships, of work commitments, of community.

The sojourner may eventually come to a dark night of the soul when not only her old form of prayer doesn't work anymore, but even God seems to have disappeared. Even when she lets go of her old form of prayer and opens herself to listen for something new, there doesn't seem to be any new path opening to God. It is in this time that she learns to desire God for God's self, not only for what God can give her. This may be hard to understand, especially if her desires have been reshaped so much that what she desires is her own spiritual transformation. This is the point at which her ego and her very life becomes relativized to a higher good, and she is able to fully let go. Of course most believers glimpse this place and live in it briefly, then slip back into a more ego-centered place. Over time, as they continue to walk the spiritual path, they can learn to live more and more fully into this place of letting go. The table below summarizes this path:

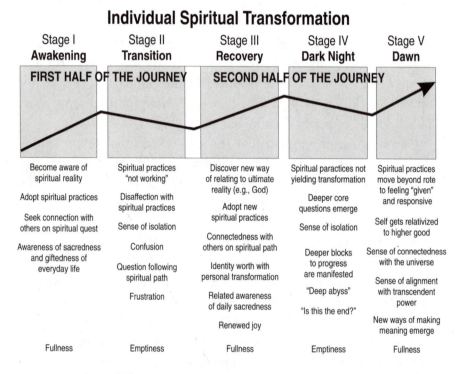

Individual Spiritual Transformation

Stage I Awakening	Stage II Transition	Stage III Recovery	Stage IV Dark Night	Stage V Dawn
FIRST HALF OF THE JOURNEY		SECOND HALF OF THE JOURNEY		
Become aware of spiritual reality	Spiritual practices "not working"	Discover new way of relating to ultimate reality (e.g., God)	Spiritual paractices not yielding transformation	Spiritual practices move beyond rote to feeling "given" and responsive
Adopt spiritual practices	Disaffection with spiritual practices	Adopt new spiritual practices	Deeper core questions emerge	
Seek connection with others on spiritual quest	Sense of isolation	Connectedness with others on spiritual path	Sense of isolation	Self gets relativized to higher good
Awareness of sacredness and giftedness of everyday life	Confusion	Identity worth with personal transformation	Deeper blocks to progress are manifested	Sense of connectedness with the universe
	Question following spiritual path		"Deep abyss"	Sense of alignment with transcendent power
	Frustration	Related awareness of daily sacredness	"Is this the end?"	
		Renewed joy		New ways of making meaning emerge
Fullness	Emptiness	Fullness	Emptiness	Fullness

Spiritual teachers through the ages have articulated the unfolding of this spiritual path. In so doing, they help the sojourner understand what is occurring when she experiences it herself or when she sees it in those she accompanies spiritually. Because a spiritual guide knows what is happening when a sojourner's first "gimme" prayers don't make it "past the ceiling," she can suggest that perhaps God is inviting her into a new form of prayer and help her be open to that. When the first exhilaration of being in love with God begins to fade, a spiritual guide can help a sojourner see the invitation to build a more solid love relationship with God, just as in a marriage when the initial romantic exhilaration begins to fade.

ORGANIZATIONAL TRANSFORMATION

Just as with individual spirituality, an organization often embraces spirituality because it needs help. And often it gets the help it was seeking. It becomes more energized, more joy-filled, and even more profitable, because it has embraced spirituality. At the same time, starting down a spiritual path will take the organization to unexpected places. The organization will eventually bump into a wall that can, if the organization is willing, serve as an invitation to the second half of the journey.

In order to understand what this transition to the second half of the journey looks like in an organization, let's return to Reell Precision Manufacturing. As we saw in chapter 8, in 1972, two years after Reell had incorporated with three employees and very little capital, the company made explicit its commitment to "follow the will of God" in business decisions. They also committed themselves to other spiritual principles, to "do what is right, even when it does not seem to be profitable, expedient, or conventional" and to "treat the concerns of others, for example, employees, customers, and suppliers, equally with our own concerns." By 1974 they were experiencing the fruits of faithfully following spiritual principles, enjoying record sales, and growing the company to ten people. Reell was a shining example of how integrating spirituality into an organization improves organizational performance. The rewards of the first half of the journey were theirs.

Then, as we saw in chapter 8, in 1975 "the roof fell in." Recall that for an individual the transition to the second half of the journey often occurs when "the roof falls in," when the abundant gifts the individual has been receiving in response to prayer and other spiritual practices dry up. Such turned out to be the case for Reell. Just as an individual can either abandon the spiritual path when the gifts dry up or choose to listen for God's guidance and deepen, so too an organization has a choice. As noted in chapter 8, Reell chose to seek God's guidance and deepen. As an individual seeking God's guidance learns to listen and respond, so can an organization. As an individual gradually learns that the spiritual journey is not about getting what one wants but rather is about one's transformation, so can an organization. Reell learned both.

The seeds of Reell's transformation were sown by two events in 1975, early in the company's history. First, as we saw in chapter 8, Reell sought God's guidance in 1975 and made the important decision not to do layoffs. This decision planted the seed of Reell's subsequent philosophy that made the security and growth of employees the highest priority of the company.

Second, Reell faced a research-and-development challenge. Their new customer issued them a challenge to design a new clutch for an application different from the one for which they were already using Reell's product. Though the usual business practice would be to cut R & D during a recession, Reell again chose a different path. Again through practicing corporate spiritual discernment, seeking God's will, the three owners decided to devote time and money to the development of the new product. Within a month they demonstrated a prototype to the customer. With several years' further development, Reell's radial electric clutch set the performance standard of the industry. The seed of Reell's philosophy of utilizing excess human resources for R & D during a recession rather than cutting excess resources to increase short-term profits had been planted.

Reell had made the transition from the first half of the journey to the second. When the roof fell in, they turned to God and learned to listen for God's guidance. Through listening and responding, they began to learn that the spiritual path was more about their transformation than it was about God fulfilling their desires.

As the years went by, Reell continued to experience deepening transformation. The process of spiritual growth continued to cycle around: abundance followed by a dry spell, followed by seeking God's guidance, followed by new direction emerging, resulting in deepening transformation.

For example, the commitment to employees (or co-workers, as Reell had begun to call them by then) was further deepened by articulating Reell's Direction Statement regarding the role of profits:

> We recognize that profitability is necessary to continue the business, reach our full potential and fulfill our responsibilities to shareholders, but our commitments to co-workers and customers come before short-term profits.[76]

When another dry spell came in the late 1970s, this statement was understood to mean that profits would be taken down to zero before a layoff would be considered. Furthermore, cuts in hours worked or salary were again requested, with the co-owners again taking even larger cuts. Again, morale remained high, and new growth emerged once sales of the electric clutch took off. The commitment to co-workers had been tested twice and was now deeply in place.

In 1983 further transformation occurred when once again Reell found itself up against a wall. This time, manufacturing processes that had worked well when the company was smaller no longer worked. The inspection process had grown unwieldy, valuable time was being wasted, and manufacturing workers grew increasingly frustrated. The problem grew out of the setup and inspection process that had been instituted earlier — a manufacturing team would set up the process and produce a few samples of a new item, an independent inspector from quality control would inspect and approve the samples, and then the job could be run. Because inspectors often were not available for several hours, too much time elapsed between the initial setup and the job being run, especially in cases where the process required several iterations of setup, inspection, and adjustment. Perhaps because of the valuing of co-workers that had already become part of the company's culture, someone suggested, "What if we taught the setup people to do their own inspection and trusted them to do it right?"

Instead of providing for more control when the company grew, the decision was made to trust the co-workers and let go of control. The seeds of another transformation had been planted.

Reell found that the results surprised them. The quality of production improved. "This was the first step in a philosophical evolution from a Plan-Direct-Control style of management to a Teach-Equip-Trust style.... Greater productivity, better quality, and growth for the individual were achieved," reported Bob Wahlstedt. Because of Reell's positive experience on a small scale, they were willing to try just-in-time (JIT) manufacturing when exposed to it by Xerox shortly thereafter. The JIT techniques proved to be just what Reell needed to extend the Teach-Equip-Trust philosophy to their entire manufacturing operation. These changes transformed the company. Not only was the company transformed, but also the owners and managers discovered something important about what they had been taught about managing a manufacturing business. Bob Wahlstedt reported, "This revolution has shown us that the biggest misconception of American manufacturers is the belief that production workers are not dependable and must be motivated and/or constrained to do quality work. We have been amazed by the self-motivation and dedication to quality and productivity that they demonstrate when they are freed to develop and use their full potential."

As we saw in chapter 8, the 1990s saw transformation of yet a different sort. When some co-workers felt excluded by the phrase "to follow the will of God" and when Reell's corporate discernment process yielded another formulation of Reell's Direction Statement, the company found itself even more firmly rooted in its spiritual principles and practices, albeit with different language. The relevant part of the Direction Statement now read:

> RPM is a team dedicated to the purpose of operating a business based on the practical application of Judeo-Christian values for the mutual benefit of *co-workers and their families, customers, shareholders, suppliers, and community.* We are committed to provide an environment where there is harmony between work and our moral/ethical values and family responsibilities and where everyone is treated justly.

The tradition of excellence at RPM was founded on a commitment to excellence rooted in the character of our Creator. Instead of driving each other toward excellence, we strive to free each other to grow and express the excellence that is within all of us. By adhering to the following principles, we are challenged to work and make decisions consistent with God's purpose for creation according to our individual understanding.

DO WHAT IS RIGHT. We are committed to do what is right even when it does not seem to be profitable, expedient, or conventional.

DO OUR BEST. In our understanding of excellence we embrace a commitment to continuous improvement in everything we do. It is our commitment to encourage, teach, equip, and free each other to do and become all that we were intended to be.

TREAT OTHERS AS WE WOULD LIKE TO BE TREATED.

SEEK INSPIRATIONAL WISDOM by looking outside ourselves, especially with respect to decisions having far-reaching and unpredictable consequences, but we will act only when the action is confirmed unanimously by others concerned.[77]

Thus, once again Reell found that hitting the wall led to deeper transformation, when the challenge was met with openness and discernment. The apparent problem became an opportunity for deepening. The wall became a window through which Reell saw itself more clearly and learned to reflect more clearly to itself and the world what it is. The inclusiveness the company was already practicing found words in the statement of identity.

Having seen Reell's transition to the second half of the journey and its ongoing transformation over the years, let us now move to the deepest level of transformation. Recall that for an individual the deepest level of transformation occurs when a person learns to want God for God's self rather than for the gifts God gives, even when the gifts are about the person's transformation (see the table on p. 136). It is here that ego dies and the self gets relativized to the higher good. Most people who move to this level of transformation slip in and out of it, gradually learning to dwell there more fully. An organization can experience something similar.

In the case of Reell, this deepest level of transformation has always been an ideal to which to aspire. Reell has, since its early days, attempted to seek the good for the sake of the good, not just for the rewards it would bring — for example, "Do what is right even when it does not seem profitable, expedient, or conventional." Two examples illustrate how Reell has begun to actualize this deepest level of transformation, seeking the good for the sake of the good, allowing the organization and its existence to be relativized to the service of the good.

The roots of this deepest level of transformation go back to the mid-1980s, when an insurance agent brought a problem to the attention of the three cofounders. He suggested buying additional insurance so that when one of the cofounders died, the other two would be able to buy out his share of the company. Among other problems the cofounders found with this proposal was that when the last cofounder died, the company would be sold to the highest bidder. They realized they didn't want the company to survive just for the sake of surviving. The only reason for the company to survive would be if it could continue to serve the higher purposes in the world that it had been serving. Thus, they devised an unconventional plan to gradually transfer ownership of the company to the people who would be most likely to carry on its mission and values: their children (through gifts of company stock) and the Reell co-workers (through an employee stock ownership plan). By the end of the decade, two-thirds of the company had been transferred to these people. While the founders realized they couldn't guarantee that the company would continue to serve the higher good, they wanted to do everything they could to increase the odds of this occurring. In their eyes, what was most important was the higher good; the company should continue to exist only if doing so would serve that higher good.

The second example comes from the 1990s. Steve Wikstrom, now co-CEO of Reell, states the orientation of the company: "What is the company here for in the biggest sense? What are we in this for? What's the big picture? What do we hope to have accomplished when we look back?" As an illustration, he tells a story:

The president of our company heard a senior officer of a large corporation talk at a seminar about total quality and empowerment. He asked the speaker later, "Do you think that what you are doing is motivated primarily by a sense of enlightened self-interest or by something bigger and higher than that?" The speaker thought about it for awhile and said, "Probably enlightened self-interest." At that point our president asked him, "What do you think will happen when the chips are down, when the competition is stiff, when you are losing money? Do you think you will stand by those elements of total quality that had to do with empowerment and building people and those kinds of things?" The man replied, "I don't know if we will."[78]

Wikstrom makes the point that one's motivation has to be more than enlightened self-interest. Reell, he believes, has turned that corner and reoriented itself to a higher purpose:

If you asked people around here, "What's the worst thing that could happen?" going out of business would not be the number-one response. I believe they would say, to abandon the "north" [the higher purpose] that we have defined on the compass. If we were to abandon that, I know the people I work with would say, "Pull the plug on it and walk away. It's not that important to us."[79]

The organization as a whole, for the most part, has let go of its survival instinct as the driving force in decision making. The higher good has become the focus and in so doing has relativized the organization.

The table on the following page summarizes the process of organizational transformation as illustrated by Reell, parallel to the process of individual transformation summarized in the table on p. 136.

CONCLUSION

How does understanding the second half of the journey help answer the difficult questions raised at the beginning of the chapter — that is, reconciling the impulse to demonstrate that spirituality improves organizational performance with the impulse to argue for the value of organizational spirituality completely apart from demonstrable financial gains? Further, how does understanding the second half of the journey help leaders who walk with their organizations through spiritual growth?

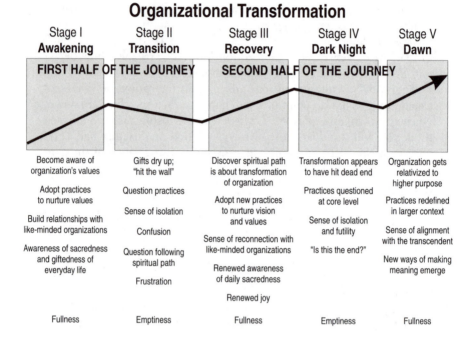

Organizational Transformation

Stage I Awakening	Stage II Transition	Stage III Recovery	Stage IV Dark Night	Stage V Dawn
FIRST HALF OF THE JOURNEY		SECOND HALF OF THE JOURNEY		
Become aware of organization's values	Gifts dry up; "hit the wall"	Discover spiritual path is about transformation of organization	Transformation appears to have hit dead end	Organization gets relativized to higher purpose
Adopt practices to nurture values	Question practices	Adopt new practices to nurture vision and values	Practices questioned at core level	Practices redefined in larger context
Build relationships with like-minded organizations	Sense of isolation	Sense of reconnection with like-minded organizations	Sense of isolation and futility	Sense of alignment with the transcendent
Awareness of sacredness and giftedness of everyday life	Confusion	Renewed awareness of daily sacredness	"Is this the end?"	New ways of making meaning emerge
	Question following spiritual path	Renewed joy		
	Frustration			
Fullness	Emptiness	Fullness	Emptiness	Fullness

First, it helps leaders understand that even though the spiritual path is not ultimately about enlightened self-interest, most individuals and organizations begin the spiritual journey at that point. This is a natural starting point, and there is nothing wrong with seeking spirituality for "selfish" reasons. At the same time, if they continue on the spiritual path, they eventually reach a different place. They learn that the spiritual journey is about their transformation rather than about the material gain they can procure from it. They ultimately learn that self-preservation is not the highest good, experiencing the relativization of self and organization to a higher purpose. Thus, rather than worrying about organizations starting on the spiritual path for the "wrong" reason, that is, to enhance organizational performance, leaders need to recognize this as a natural starting point for a spiritual journey, for individuals and for organizations. Then they can refocus their attention on the inevitable bumps organizations will encounter, and in particular on how to help them through the transition to the second half of the journey.

Second, it helps leaders know how to guide organizations on the second half of the journey. Just as spiritual guides help individuals on the second half of the journey by understanding and pointing out the recurring cycles of spiritual challenge and growth, so can leaders help organizations on the second half of the journey. When leaders understand the process of spiritual growth in organizations, they can help normalize what an organization is experiencing and point it toward examples of others who have traveled the path before them. This way each organization seeking to follow a spiritual path doesn't have to reinvent the wheel when it encounters the inevitable challenges of the second half of the journey. Spiritual guides for organizations, like spiritual guides for individuals, can draw on the collective wisdom of others' experience and compassionately walk with organizations through their transformation. While such companionship may not make the process any easier, at least it demystifies the process and lets the organization know it is not alone but that it is surrounded by a cloud of witnesses who have hit the bumps, clambered over them, and made it through to the other side.

Conclusion

PUTTING SOUL TO WORK IN YOUR ORGANIZATION

꒰ ꒱

How might *your* organization exhibit soul at work? You've seen soul at work through a variety of leaders in a variety of settings. You've seen it in business, in health care, in nonprofits, in the arts. What does it all mean for you? In the words of Jean Quinn at Sophia Housing, "We are all leaders." Whatever your sphere of influence, large or small, you can put soul to work in your organization.

This chapter summarizes the themes of the book. Recognizing that a strong inner life provides the foundation for spiritually grounded leadership, the chapter begins with a recap of the inner lives of the four leaders examined in depth in part 1, considering how their spiritual practices sustain them, and drawing lessons from them about spiritual sustenance for you as a leader in your sphere. The chapter then moves to a recap of part 2, considering how spirituality gets integrated into the organization as a whole in the organizations we have considered, and drawing lessons from them about how you can integrate spirituality into your organization.

SUSTAINING SPIRITUALLY GROUNDED LEADERSHIP

Whatever your sphere of influence, you will be a more effective leader if you are more spiritually grounded. As a leader, you can learn from the leaders whose stories this book has told. Though different in many ways, the leaders share three commonalities: they all bring their souls to work, they all have discovered ways of sustaining their souls in the midst of the daily pressures of the workplace, and they all bring their spiritually grounded presence into their sphere of influence. Genny Nelson, Bob Carlson, Theresa McCoy, and Joe Clubb, the leaders highlighted in part 1, all maintain regular spiritual practices, both inside and outside of their workplaces, in order to keep themselves centered in the midst of the daily challenges they face. While they all experience being knocked off balance at times, and they all acknowledge the daily struggle to stay spiritually grounded, they all have found ways to regain their balance when they falter and to more or less stay in touch with their spiritual center and their moral compass. They have all discovered spiritual practices that work for them. While spiritual practices vary among particular individuals, and while they change for an individual over time, four commonalities stand out. To maximize spiritual groundedness in their roles, leaders need (1) individual spiritual practices (a) outside the workplace and (b) inside the workplace, and (2) spiritual community (a) outside the workplace and (b) inside the workplace. Let's examine each of these in turn, with illustrations from the four leaders in part 1.

1a. *Individual spiritual practices outside the workplace.* Genny Nelson gets away to pray at the downtown chapel when she needs perspective and encouragement for the challenges of Sisters of the Road Café. She also keeps a regular practice of journaling. Bob Carlson of Reell Precision Manufacturing relies on such practices as walking in nature and listening to music for his spiritual nurture.

1b. *Individual spiritual practices inside the workplace.* Genny Nelson maintains a running conversation with God throughout the day, praying for strength, guidance, and courage. She also practices nonviolence daily at Sisters, meeting violence with consistency, firmness, and love. Theresa McCoy, we observed, closed her door, rang her bell, and did her prayers and chanting in her office when she needed to regain strength and perspective for her work at Greyston Family Support Services. She also exercised self-reflection when she found herself judging someone, discovering how opinionated she herself was when she judged another as opinionated.

2a. *Spiritual community outside the workplace.* Bob Carlson draws on the corporate worship at his Protestant church to help feed his soul. Joe Clubb of HealthEast serves as cantor and participates in worship at his Roman Catholic parish. Theresa McCoy relies on the spiritual support of her Soka Gakkai International (SGI) center, the local Buddhist community of practice.

2b. *Spiritual community inside the workplace.* Bob Carlson experiences spiritual community in the workplace in the Tuesday morning breakfast meetings in which the three leaders "seek inspirational wisdom" together. He also finds spiritual nurture in board meetings. Theresa McCoy found spiritual community in such places as the Greyston leadership team meetings where her colleagues would encourage her to pray about her challenges. She also experienced spiritual nurture through the Way of Council as it was practiced in leadership team meetings. Joe Clubb finds spiritual community in the workplace through the sharing at ICP meetings, as well as through asking colleagues to pray for him in difficult workplace challenges. The table on the following page summarizes these four commonalities and examples.

Being a spiritually grounded leader is difficult to sustain alone. Like these leaders, you can maintain spiritual practices both inside and outside the workplace, and you can seek spiritual community both inside and outside the workplace. These leaders are fortunate in that they find spiritual community within their organizations as well as outside. If you are a leader in an organization without much explicit spirituality, you will need to strengthen the other three quadrants and, at the same time, begin to pray that you will see where else in your organization soul is at work. As you venture out and mention to colleagues that you, say, attended a particular workshop or read a particular book, you may be surprised to discover kindred spirits. Jean Quinn and Eamonn Martin of Sophia Housing discovered one another in this way when they worked together at their previous place of employment. You may then find that you can build on what you have together to influence a certain sector of your organization, or even, perhaps, over several years, as Joe Clubb discovered, you can be part of a ripple effect throughout many sectors of the organization. You may find, as Jean Quinn and Eamonn Martin eventually did, that

	Outside workplace	Inside workplace
Individual Spiritual Practice	Genny: Journaling Praying at downtown chapel Bob: Walking in nature Listening to music	Genny: Running conversation with God Meeting violence with firmness and love Theresa: Praying/chanting in office Self-reflection
Spiritual Community	Bob: Protestant church worship Joe: Catholic Mass at local parish Theresa: Buddhist SGI Center	Bob: Tuesday AM breakfast meetings, seeking "inspirational wisdom" together Board meetings Theresa: Leadership team meetings using Way of Council Joe: ICP meetings Asking colleagues to pray

there comes a point at which you need to leave your current organization in order to spread your wings and influence an organization more broadly to integrate spirituality throughout its life.

With this summary of spiritually grounded leadership as a foundation, let's consider in more detail how to nurture spirituality within an organization.

ORGANIZATION AS A WHOLE

The businesses, health-care organizations, and nonprofits we saw in part 2, though very different, all share several commonalities. Organizations that keep their souls thriving do so primarily in five ways: (1) they attend to soul in their official documents, (2) they hire for congruence with their mission, (3) they devote time and attention to nurturing organizational soul, (4) they dedicate personnel to the task, and (5) they create specific structures and processes that nurture the soul of the organization. This section considers each of these five ways in turn, providing illustrations from the organizations examined in part 2.

First, the organizations attend to soul in their official documents. In its Direction Statement, for example, Reell Precision Manufacturing articulates its commitment to "seek inspirational wisdom," "do what is right," and "provide an environment where there is harmony between work and our moral/ethical values and family responsibilities and where everyone is treated justly." Document Management Group's vision statement includes a commitment to build a workplace in which "our people can find meaning, significance and success through their work, and where personal and workplace values align to achieve greater outward harmony and inner spiritual life." Sisters of the Road Café "exists to build authentic relationships and alleviate the hunger of isolation in an atmosphere of nonviolence and gentle personalism that nurtures the whole individual." Sophia Housing "is a weaving of holistic support for marginalized people to enable them to become aware of their own inner strength and potential." Our Lady's Hospice "strives in an atmosphere of loving care to promote wholeness of body, mind and spirit."

Second, once having articulated their values, organizations hire for congruence with the mission. Southwest Airlines, committed to creating a fun, caring environment for employees and customers, hires for attitude first and then trains for skills. Sophia Housing, committed to a holistic approach of helping "marginalized people . . . become aware of their own inner strengths and potential," hires people (even while hiring for positions like bookkeeper or caterer, whose relevance to the mission might not be readily apparent) who share that vision and who seek to grow holistically and build relationships themselves even while they are serving the clients of Sophia Housing. Our Lady's Hospice hires nurses who are committed to offering "loving care," as well as technical medical expertise. Shalem hires employees, including finance experts and office assistants, who share a vision of practicing and teaching contemplative prayer.

Third, they give time and attention to nurturing organizational soul. Southwest Airlines, for example, provides extensive training and ongoing support to help its employees succeed in building a fun, caring atmosphere. Document Management Group developed its Excellence through People program and its Best Companies initiative to increase employee participation in visioning and creative problem-solving and to help employees feel cared about and supported. HealthEast uses ICP, providing interdisciplinary teams the opportunity to build relationships with one another, enhance the work environment, and improve patient care, demonstrating its "passion for caring and service."

Fourth, closely related to giving time and attention, these organizations dedicate personnel to the task. Southwest Airlines maintains the highest supervisor-to-frontline-employee ratio of any airline, thus ensuring ongoing support for its mission. Furthermore it sponsors its University for People, paying a full-time director and liberating others to teach as part of their job descriptions. Mercy Medical devotes a full-time position to the mission leader, who sits on the senior leadership team, and whose sole responsibility is to promote mission and ethics in the organization. HealthEast dedicates part of a senior manager's time to directing the ICP program, and also frees part of other employees' time to serve on the ICP council. HealthEast also employs a full-time vice president for spiritual care.

Fifth, the organizations under our consideration create structures and processes that nurture soul at work. Greyston, for example, uses the Way of Council and moments of silence in meetings throughout the organization. At Reell, the co-CEOs and other leaders use corporate spiritual discernment. Mercy Medical also uses corporate discernment through its mission discernment process. Sophia Housing builds a Wisdom Centre in every housing development and provides one-time events and ongoing groups there to help people develop their spiritual lives. Shalem uses corporate discernment in its meetings, and uses such practices as designating someone to be a contemplative presence in the group, punctuating meetings with moments of silence at regular intervals, and passing around a prayer object to remind participants of their grounding in something greater than themselves.

The foregoing summary serves as a reminder that different practices are appropriate for different organizations. Different leaders and different organizations manifest soul at work in different ways. There is no "one size fits all." Just as the leaders we saw in part 1 exercise different spiritual practices according to their individual needs and the particular time and circumstances in their lives, so the organizations integrate spirituality in different ways. Different ways are appropriate for different organizations. Different ways are appropriate for the same organization at different times.

At the same time, the five ways enumerated above surface time and again. An organization that uses all five ways will find it easier to maintain a healthy organizational soul. All of the organizations in the book use at least four of the five categories. No matter what your organization, large or small, stand-alone or a subgroup of a larger organization, you can reflect on the five ways and learn from the sample practices employed by the organizations surveyed here. The table on the following page provides a recap of the five ways and the sample practices summarized here.

GETTING FROM HERE TO THERE

Soul at work doesn't happen all at once in a magical transformation. It spreads, like warmth through melting ice, through small changes and actions, sometimes in the most unlikely of places. If you are trying to enliven the soul in your organization, here are four principles to keep in mind:

1. You Are Empowered

Regardless of your position in an organization, you have a sphere of influence and can work in that sphere to nurture or reveal soul at work. In the work of soul, a line manager may sometimes have more latitude to nurture authentic soul than a CEO.

Attend to soul in official documents	**Reell:** Seek inspirational wisdom
	   Do what is right
	   Create harmony between work and moral/ethical values
	
	 Document Management Group: Personal and workplace
	   values align
	   Find meaning, significance, and success through work
	
	 Sisters of the Road Café: Build authentic relationships
	   Practice nonviolence and gentle personalism
	
	 Sophia Housing: Weave holistic support
	   Enable awareness of inner strength and potential
	
	 Our Lady's Hospice: Create atmosphere of loving care
	   Promote wholeness of body, mind, and spirit

Hire for congruence with mission	**Southwest Airlines:** Hire for attitude, train for skills
	
	 Sophia Housing: Seek employees who desire holistic
	   growth and relationship-building for themselves
	
	 Our Lady's Hospice: Hire for ability to offer "loving care"
	   as well as technical expertise
	
	 Shalem: Seek employees who share vision of practicing
	   and teaching contemplative prayer

Devote time and attention to nurturing organizational soul	**Southwest Airlines:** Thorough training
	   Ongoing support
	
	 Document Management Group: Excellence through People
	   program
	   Best Companies initiative
	
	 HealthEast: ICP program

Dedicate personnel to the task	**Southwest Airlines:** More supervisors
	   University for People director, teachers
	
	 Mercy Medical: mission leader
	
	 HealthEast: ICP director, council
	   VP for Spiritual Care

Create specific structures and processes that nurture the soul of the organization	**Greyston:** Way of Council
	   Moments of silence
	
	 Reell: Corporate discernment
	
	 Mercy Medical: Mission discernment process
	
	 Sophia Housing: Wisdom Centres and programs
	
	 Shalem: Moments of silence in meetings
	   Prayer object
	   Designated pray-er
	   Ringing bell

2. Listen for Soul

Soul has a way of cropping up naturally within organizations. You can notice and name those places where soul crops up, and thus complement your other efforts to nurture soul. Keep in mind that pride in workmanship or joy in work are manifestations of soul at work and can provide openings to celebrate the human spirit.

3. Don't Go It Alone

Enlist partners, both within and outside of your organization, to help you think (and pray, if that is part of your tradition) about your enlivening work. Remember that soul at work transcends religious traditions, and boldly reach out across faiths while holding on to what makes you strong.

4. Patience in Peril

At times, nurturing soul at work and staying spiritually grounded will be difficult. Those difficult times are the very times it is most important to be patient and faithful. In the stories in this book, soul came to the fore most fully when organizations faced peril. Soul is important all the time, but it is most desperately needed when times are worst. Stay the course.

At the Beginning

If you've reached this point in this book, you care. You care about your organization and you care about soul and you care about bringing them together. Just as when there's a tender tree shoot, there's promise of the mature tree, so when there is care, there is hope. You have hope that you can make a difference, that you can bring soul into your work. Your caring and your hope provide the seeds of promise for the tree to be planted and grow. The ground is fertile and the seeds are ready. Start digging!

NOTES

1. This definition has a long and noble pedigree. See Mary Frohlich, "Spiritual Discipline, Discipline of Spirituality," *Spiritus* 1, no. 1 (2001) for a similar definition that draws on Bernard Lonergan, who in turn draws on Thomas Aquinas.

2. Spiritual writers use "soul" to speak not about something a person has but about who a person most deeply is. See Gerald May, *Dark Night of the Soul* (San Francisco: HarperSanFrancisco, 2004), 42. I am using "soul" here to refer not only to the individual person and who he or she most deeply is, but also to organizations and who they most deeply are. For a similar discussion, see Tom Chappell, *The Soul of a Business* (New York: Bantam, 1996), in which he uses "soul of a business" to refer to the set of shared values and vision that are at the core of a business organization.

3. See, for example, David Batstone, *Saving the Corporate Soul* (San Francisco: Jossey-Bass, 2003); Peter Cohan, *Value Leadership* (San Francisco: Jossey-Bass, 2003); Richard Wedemeyer and Ronald Jue, *The Inner Edge: Achieving Spirituality in Your Life and Work* (Chicago: McGraw-Hill, 2002); Jody Hoffer Gittell, *The Southwest Airlines Way: Using the Power of Relationships to Achieve High Performance* (New York: McGraw-Hill, 2003); Douglas K. Smith, *On Value and Values: Thinking Differently about We in the Age of Me* (Upper Saddle River, N.J.: Prentice Hall, 2004); Robert B. Catell, Kenny Moore, and Glenn Rifkin, *The CEO and the Monk: One Company's Journey to Profit and Purpose* (Hoboken, N.J.: Wiley, 2004); and Marc Gunther, *Faith and Fortune: The Quiet Revolution to Reform American Business* (New York: Crown Business, 2004).

4. Bob Wahlstedt, Reell Precision Manufacturing. See also a similar definition of profit in James C. Collins and Jerry I. Porras, *Built to Last: Successful Habits of Visionary Companies* (New York: HarperBusiness, 1994).

5. *Newsday,* March 1, 2004, 4.

6. HealthEast vision statement.

7. For example, Continental Lite and United Shuttle.

8. Jody Hoffer Gittell, *The Southwest Airlines Way: Using the Power of Relationships to Achieve High Performance* (New York: McGraw-Hill, 2003), 85–100.

9. As of April 17, 2005, Southwest Airlines' market capitalization was $11.6 billion, and the many other U.S. airlines' market capitalization combined was less than $8 billion.

10. See the introduction for a definition of organizational soul, especially note 2 above.

11. ICP is a trademarked program created by Bonnie Wesorick from Grand Rapids, Mich. See note 41.

12. Paul Nutt, "Surprising but True: Half the Decisions in Organizations Fail," *Academy of Management Executive* 13 (1999): 75–90. See also Nutt, *Why Decisions Fail: Avoiding the Blunders and Traps That Lead to Debacles* (San Francisco: Berrett-Koehler, 2002).

13. Ronald Heifetz, *Leadership without Easy Answers* (Cambridge, Mass.: Harvard/Belknap, 1994). See also Ronald Heifetz and Martin Linsky, *Leadership on the Line: Staying Alive through the Dangers of Leadership* (Cambridge, Mass.: Harvard University Press, 2002), for a thorough discussion of the dangers of leadership.

14. Paul Nutt's extensive studies over the past twenty-five years use as the primary indicator of success whether a decision is put to use long-term (Nutt, "Surprising but True," 77) See note 12.

15. Nutt, *Why Decisions Fail*, xv.

16. For more on corporate discernment, see chapter 8.

17. Aristotle, *Nicomachean Ethics* (Cambridge: Cambridge University Press, 2000).

18. Tejadhammo Bhikku, "Some Aspects of Spiritual Direction within a Living Buddhist Tradition," in *Tending the Holy: Spiritual Direction across Traditions,* ed. Norvene Vest (Harrisburg, Pa.: Morehouse, 2003), 6.

19. Christopher Key Chapple, "The Guru and Spiritual Direction," in *Tending the Holy,* ed. Vest, 36.

20. Andrew Wilson, ed., *World Scripture* (New York: Paragon House, 1991), 382.

21. Fariha al-Jerrahi, "The Sufi Path of Guidance," in *Tending the Holy,* ed. Vest, 23.

22. Suzanne G. Farnham, *Listening Hearts: Discerning Call in Community* (Harrisburg, Pa.: Morehouse, 2001), 30–34.

23. Ibid., 36–37.

24. Nutt, "Surprising but True," and Nutt, *Why Decisions Fail*.

25. André L. Delbecq, Elizabeth Liebert, SNJM, John Mostyn, CSC, Gordan Walter, and Paul Nutt, "Discernment and Strategic Decision Making: Reflections for a Spirituality of Organizational Leadership," in *Spiritual Intelligence at Work,* ed. Moses L. Pava (Amsterdam and London: Elsevier, 2004), 139–74.

26. Nutt, "Surprising but True."

27. Delbecq et al., "Discernment and Strategic Decision Making," 166.

28. Upon her retirement, Bailey founded QVF Partners, a consulting firm designed to help businesses practice the principles she practiced at Southwest Airlines.

29. Kevin and Jackie Freiberg, *Nuts! Southwest Airlines' Crazy Recipe for Business and Personal Success* (New York: Broadway Books, 1998), 268.

30. Ibid., 270.

31. Jody Hoffer Gittell, *The Southwest Airlines Way: Using the Power of Relationships to Achieve High Performance* (New York: McGraw-Hill, 2003), 3.

32. *Newsday,* March 1, 2004.

33. Ibid.

34. Greyston Foundation, "Guiding Principles," 6.

35. Ibid., 7.

36. *Newsday,* March 1, 2004.

37. Ibid.

38. Greyston Foundation, "Guiding Principles," 8.

39. Ibid., 10.

40. Interdisciplinary Clinical Practice (ICP) Manual, 5.

41. Bonnie Wesorick, Laurie Shiparski, Michelle Troseth, and Kathy Wyngarden, *Partnership Council Field Book: Strategies and Tools for Co-Creating a Healthy Work Place* (Grand Rapids, Mich.: Practice Field, 1997).

42. ICP Manual, 5.

43. Ibid.

44. Ibid., 17.

45. Ibid., 10.

46. Ibid., 13.

47. Kelly Putnam, "Depression: The Important Health Promotion Topic No One Talks About," *AWHP's Worksite Health* (Summer 2001): 33.

48. Marcus Buckingham and Curt Coffman, *First, Break All the Rules: What the World's Greatest Managers Do Differently* (New York: Simon & Schuster, 1999).

49. Putnam, "Depression," 32–33.

50. Donal S. Blake, *Mary Aikenhead: Servant of the Poor* (Dublin: Caritas, 2001), x.

51. Ibid., 54.

52. Our Lady's Hospice Mission booklet, 4.

53. Michael Kearney, *Mortally Wounded: Stories of Soul Pain, Death, and Healing* (New York: Scribner's, 1996), 15.

54. Ibid., 15, 17.

55. Tilden Edwards, *Shalem News* (Fall 2000).

56. Diane Paras, *Shalem News* (Winter 1996).

57. Patricia Clark, *Shalem News* (Winter 1996).

58. Paras, *Shalem News*.

59. Since most of the literature on spiritual discernment uses theistic language, and since two of the three illustrative cases used in this chapter used theistic language, this chapter also uses it in articulating corporate spiritual discernment. At the same time, it is important to note that a parallel description of the process could be given in nontheistic language.

60. Bob Wahlstedt, *The History of RPM* (internal RPM publication, 1989), 5–6.

61. Ibid., 6.

62. Ibid.

63. Ibid., 7.

64. Quoted in Margaret Lulic, *Who We Could Be at Work* (Minneapolis: Blue Edge, 1994), 10.

65. *Mission Discernment* (Trinity Health, 2001).

66. Ibid., 1.

67. Ibid., 2.

68. Ibid., 4.

69. Greyston Web site: www.greyston.org.

70. Dinah Wakeford, "Healing Society, Healing Ourselves at Greyston Bakery," *Fieldnotes: A Newsletter of the Shambhala Institute*, March 2004, 4.

71. Ibid.

72. Ibid., 2.

73. Ibid.

74. Nutt, "Surprising but True," and Nutt, *Why Decisions Fail.*

75. See, for example, Ken Wilber, Jack Engler, and Daniel P. Brown, *Transformations of Consciousness: Conventional and Contemplative Perspectives on Development* (Boston: Shambhala, 1986), and Jack Kornfield, *After the Ecstasy, the Laundry* (New York: Bantam, 2001).

76. Reell Precision Manufacturing Direction Statement.

77. 1992 Direction Statement, emphases in original.

Reell's current Direction Statement (revised in 2004) reads:

Reell is a team united in the operation of a business based on the practical application of spiritual values to promote the growth of individuals and advance the common good for the benefit of co-workers and their families, customers, shareholders, suppliers and community. Rooted in Judeo-Christian values, we welcome and draw on the richness of our spiritually diverse community. We are committed to provide an environment where there is harmony between work and our moral/ethical values and family responsibilities and where everyone is treated justly.

The tradition of excellence at Reell was founded on a commitment to excellence rooted in the character of our Creator. Instead of driving each other toward excellence, we strive to free each other to grow and express the excellence that is within all of us.

By adhering to the following four common spiritual principles, we are challenged to work and make decisions consistent with God's purpose for creation according to our individual understanding.

Do what is right	We are committed to do what is right, even when it does not seem to be profitable, expedient, or conventional.
Do our best	In our understanding of excellence we embrace a commitment to continuous improvement in everything we do. It is our commitment to encourage, teach, equip, and free each other to do and become all that we were intended to be.
Treat others as we would like to be treated	
Seek Inspirational Wisdom	By looking outside ourselves, especially with respect to decisions having far-reaching and unpredictable consequences, but we will act only when the action is confirmed unanimously by others concerned.

We currently design and manufacture innovative products for a global market. Our goal is to continually improve our ability to meet customer needs. How we accomplish our mission is important to us. The following groups are fundamental to our success:

Co-workers	People are the heart of Reell. We are committed to provide a secure opportunity to earn a livelihood and pursue personal growth.
Customers	Customers are the lifeblood of Reell. Our products and services must be the best in meeting and exceeding customer expectations.
Shareholders	We recognize that profitability is necessary to continue in business, reach our full potential, and fulfill our responsibilities to shareholders. We expect profits, but our commitments to co-workers and customers come before short-term profits.

Suppliers   We will treat our suppliers as valuable partners in all our activities.

Community   We will use a share of our energy and resources to meet the needs of our local and global community.

We find that in following these principles we can experience enjoyment, happiness, and peace of mind in our work and in our individual lives.

78. Quoted in Lulic, *Who We Could Be at Work,* 14.
79. Ibid.